HOLLERS THE DODGER

THE STORY OF A SOUTH AFRICAN RACEHORSE

Sharlene Frances

PUBLICATION
CONSULTANTS
We Believe In The Power Of Authors

8370 Eleusis Drive, Anchorage, Alaska 99502-4630
books@publicationconsultants.com—www.publicationconsultants.com

ISBN Number: 978-1-63747-405-1
eBook ISBN Number: 978-1-63747-406-8

Library of Congress Number: 2024940078

Manufactured in the United States of America

DEDICATION

This book is dedicated to Hollers The Dodger and to all those warriors who cannot speak for themselves; to those who have had to endure unspeakable hardship at the hands of the merciless.

This book is also dedicated to the saviors who stand up and speak for the voiceless. Who swoop in where angels fear to tread to pluck the innocent from the clutches of hell itself.

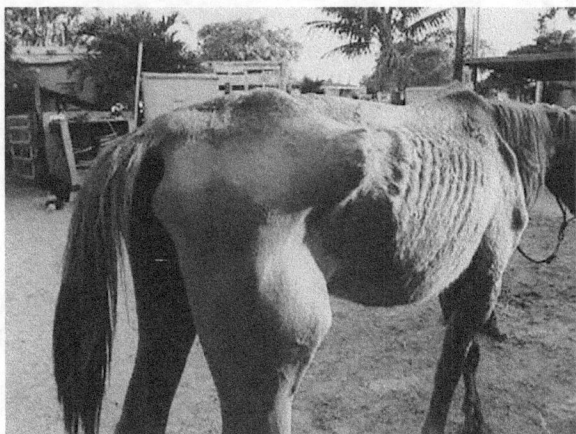

Hollers The Dodger a few weeks after he was rescued by St Romnick Equine Rescue. At the time this photo was taken, he had gained some weight and was finally able to stand.

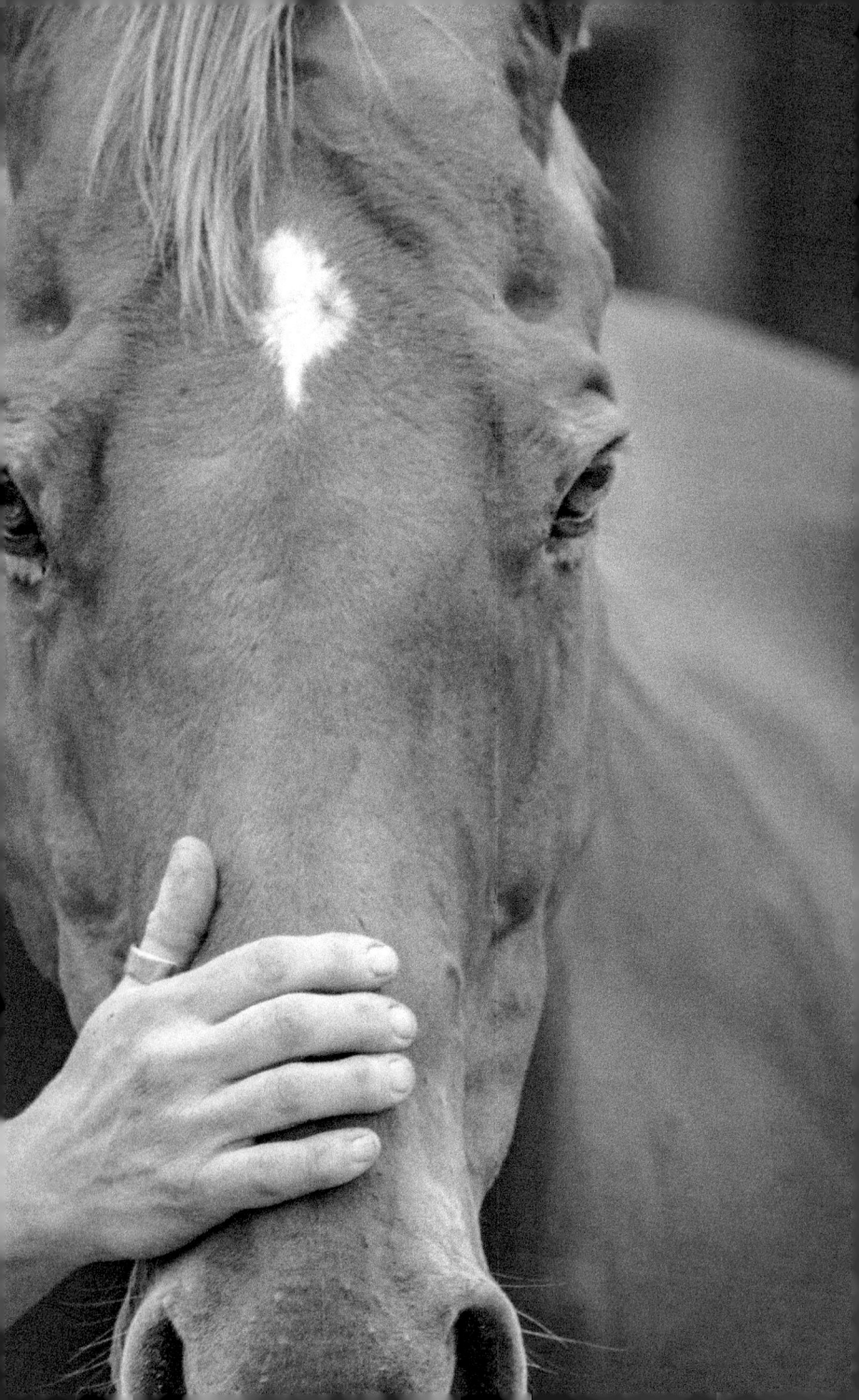

Acknowledgements

Special thanks to St Romnik Equine Rescue. They are the guardian angels without whom many horses could not have survived. They bring hope and light into shattered lives, without them, this book could not have been written.

A very special thanks to my awesome friend Fiona Rom, who so kindly took time out of her very busy life to come to my aid with her amazing editing skills.

Thank you from the bottom of my heart, Daniela Radley, for taking such wonderful care of our special boy, and for allowing me to use your photos in this book.

Anja Joubert (Through The Lense) - your photographs are beautiful. Thank you so much for taking time out of your busy schedule to spend time with Hollers, Grey mare and friends. I am truly grateful.

Thank you, Evan and the Publication Consultants team, for all your hard work and excellent advice. You are my light house in a very stormy sea.

A huge thank you to all my family for your unwavering support and encouragement, and for being my biggest fans!

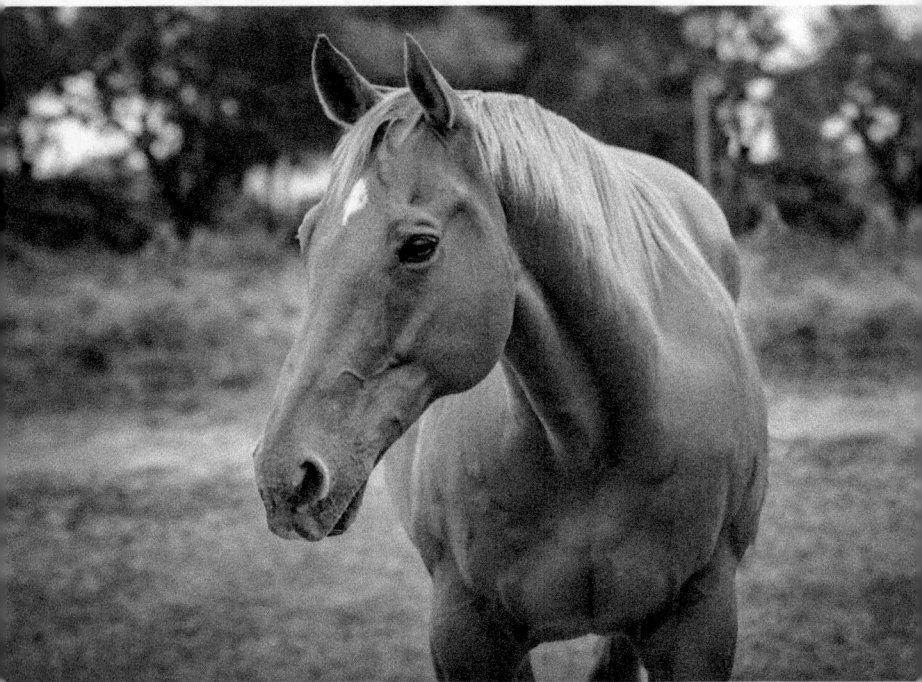

CHAPTER 1 — WOUNDED WARRIORS

"He came from nowhere.
He belongs to no one.
See that knowing in his gaze?
I will tell you what you will not see.
You will not see anger; you will not see judgement.
You will not see vengeance.
This is one of God's special creations.
And to find such a horse in the middle of this filth,
This hell on earth,
is like finding an angel caught in a web of terror.
And yet – there is still no bitterness."

I see everything through a red haze. I am beyond pain. I am beyond terror. It feels as if my heart is crashing, pounding inside my head. I hear my breath coming in heaving gasps. I look into the bloodshot, glazed eye of the one running next to me. There is none of the earlier desperation, none of the blind panic - just a blank, hopeless resignation that death is waiting. The frenzied drumming of hooves seeps into my clouded consciousness, along with the screaming of the blood-crazed monsters lining the narrow streets upon which we run. I hear the groan before I feel blood spraying into my eyes and onto my face, and the one who runs alongside me dips and plunges as her legs give way, she ploughs headlong into the burning pavement. Her scrambling feet catch my front legs and I see the broken road rushing up to meet me. Everything is black.

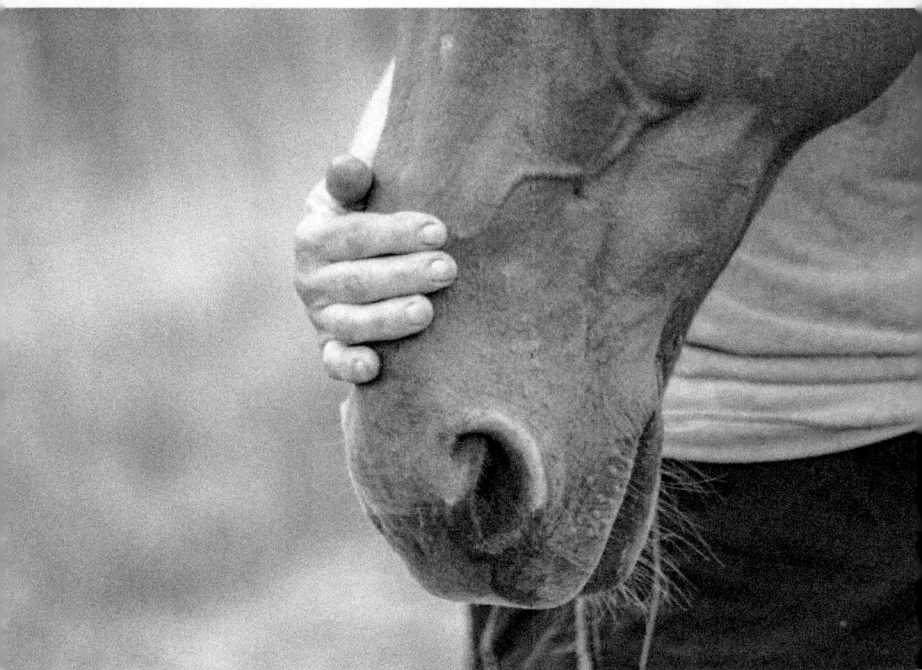

Chapter 2 – Remember

"No matter where you may be,
I will find you, my son.
I will find you.
And I will bring you home."

SHARLENE FRANCES

A familiar scent lifts me out of the darkness, but it is faint and mixed with the stronger stenches of blood, fear and death. I want to sink back into that comforting darkness, away from the overwhelming pain, away from the absolute horror of the world in which I have found myself. It is the sweet scent of happy days past, of safety and hope, that stops me from letting go and sinking back into the abyss.......

Maddi was there the day I was born. Her kind, reassuring hands helped me to stand upon my wobbly new-born legs. Her strong, safe arms prevented me from falling headlong into the stable wall. Maddi was there the first day I went outside with my mother into a grassy field to enjoy the warm sunshine. Maddi laughed when I tried showing off on my long, baby legs, my efforts far from graceful. Whenever she entered our field, the other babies and I jostled one another to be near her. When the time came to be weaned away from our mothers, Maddi was our comfort and the constant in our lives.

Maddi taught us many things from the day we were born. Her familiar voice would ring out well before breakfast time – she was a great organizer! She made sure that we were all treated well and handled with professionalism and kindness. We were champions in the making, after all; we were the next generation of racehorses destined to grace the racetracks. We were royalty, and our exciting lives were set before us. As youngsters we would run, racing one another around the fields. Fighting to be the winner. The feel of my muscles stretching and burning as I strained to get to the front was glorious! My speed was exhilarating; the wind howled in my ears as I ran, as I flew.

There is that waft of sweetness again. Not the sickening sweet smell of blood, but the light, fresh, warm smell of comfort and hope. I try to focus my eyes, try to see. My eyelids are stuck shut; they feel sticky. White-hot pain floods through my entire body as I lie broken on the roadside, in thick darkness ….

I feel the icy rain beating down on me, pinpricks of brightness stab at my eyelids. I hear the rumble and the hissing of morning traffic, the excited chatter of people.

"So much blood! How can he be alive?"

"Where is that policeman? He was here just a minute ago."

"He went to fetch the doctor – she is still busy with that dead horse at the end of the road."

"……. they have been out here all night……"

"Is this other one dead? It looks like they fell together."

The other one...... the one who was running next to me. I remember her. I remember her fright and panic. I remember her wide, rolling eyes. Her mouth ripped and bleeding before we had even started running, her gray coat was dark, dripping with sweat and blood – full of welts and cuts from that evil long whip that her rider wielded with sadistic delight.

She ran alongside me. The monster clinging to her back slashed and sliced at me with his whip. Whatever was sitting on my back (he could not have been human), grabbed at the flying whip, and we all collided. Demons upon our backs, enraged and screaming, the flash of a blade, and blood splattered......

Now lying on that freezing road, waves of terror and horror crash down on me. I smell fear, a fear that has no words. I smell death. I must escape this place! I must run! I must run! Heat surges through my broken, bloodied body. I cannot see! I cannot move! Something is heavy on my thrashing legs, something holding me down. In my blindness and panic, I am completely alone. In my blindness and panic, there is no one.........

Chapter 3 – Nobody's Horse

Where is your shimmering coat, Angel?
What happened to your long legs, your bunched muscles?
Have they clipped your wings, Angel?
Have they bound your legs?
Where is that soaring spirit?
Has it been overshadowed by this heavy stench of fear?
Ahhhh – no, I see a spark in your eye.
Better to not let it die.

SHARLENE FRANCES

There it is again; a scent that cuts through all that is dark. A voice comes from a distance, but I can hear it. A soft voice, a voice of strength, a voice of calm. Hands. Kind, warm hands on my straining neck. I feel my stiff muscles relaxing under those stroking hands and that smooth voice.

"What have they done to you, my lovely boy? I am sorry. So sorry."

The voice hardens and becomes one of authority.

"Who is the owner of this horse? Where is his owner?!"

Her question is met with stony silence. Nobody knows anything, nobody saw anything.

"Okay, let us clean you up big guy, we need to get you out of here. You will soon be feeling much better, my son."

She turns to a person standing next to her.

"Right! I need help to get this gray horse off – easy now, we must be slow and careful. Mind where you are stepping."

I hear a shuffle of feet and calm, steady voices. I realize that it is the gray mare lying on my legs. Strong hands take hold of her bloodied head and swollen legs, and they haul her off me.

"Her breathing is very shallow; I am not sure this one is going to make it. I am surprised she is alive at all."

She is alive?

"These two fell at speed; they slid along the road for quite a distance which shredded the skin off them and by the looks of these multiple wounds they have been stabbed with a large blade many times. The mare's jugular was missed by just a few centimeters. The chestnut is very thin; he is almost a skeleton really. How he even managed to run this far is beyond me – I would love to find his owner!"

There is anger and sadness in her voice. My owner – grief floods my heart. I no longer have an owner. I have been set adrift in a nightmare where there is not a shred of humanity. How did I end up here, lying in blood and freezing mud? Left for dead on the side of a back road in the middle of this squalor and poverty?

Chapter 4 – Part of The Cool Team

"There is a touch of divinity even in brutes,
And a special halo about a horse,
That should forever exempt him from indignities."

HERMAN MELVILLE

We all left the farm eventually. Most of us were sent to the sales to be sold at auction; some of us were sold privately. We were brushed and polished until our coats gleamed and we pranced proudly alongside our handlers, showing off our strength and fire. My beautiful chestnut color shone like the finest gold; I was a big, strong colt, although too long in the back in some people's opinion. I ended up leaving the farm with a few of my buddies. We were still babies at the time, not yet two years old. I remember how exciting and scary it was to walk up the ramp of that huge horsebox. Maddi was there, of course. She had a strange quietness to her voice as she spoke to each of us in turn. It never entered my mind that she would not be there on the other side, that she would be gone from my life forever. I was tall enough to stretch up and poke my nose through the small window at the top. I could just see the green paddocks and the edge of the stable block, I saw Maddi standing alone, watching as the truck started to rumble away. I called out, and a few faint replies came back as we turned onto the road and the only world I had ever known disappeared from sight.

We were taken to a pre-training center outside the city. There we learned to work with a saddle and bridle and to have a rider on our backs. As we had had a lot of handling since birth, the work came to us easily. During the day, we were put into small paddocks to relax. We did a lot of strengthening work out on the farm, plenty of trotting up and down hills to get our muscles hard and fit for the racing yards. The people were good to us, and we were well looked after.

Back in the big horsebox, this time we were off to the training stables in the city. I ended up in the yard of a well-known trainer. He looked at us one by one.

"This horse still has a lot of growing to do. He should go back to the farm for at least six months." *He eyed me from under his big hat.*

"The note in his passport says that his owner insists that he race as soon as possible," *said the assistant trainer.*

"This is Hollers the Dodger – the Deep Sleep colt? I told Mike not to send him yet. He is supposed to go back to the stud farm to do a bit more growing!"

"Mike fully agrees. He put off sending him in for as long as he could, but the .owner would not hear anything else."

"Oh yes! Mr. Rateichter. I really did not want to take on any of his horses; he is a total moron! I will speak to him myself. If this horse races now he is going to be wasted. I have seen how he moves, and it looks to me like he will have enormous potential as a three-year-old."

The big man with the big hat gave my neck a friendly pat and moved off down the row of stables.

Actually, I never knew my owner, whose name was Mr. Rateichter. I had never seen him, but he was going to have a massive impact on my life, nonetheless.

Even though I was supposed to go back to the farm, there must have been some compromise agreed between owner and trainer and I ended up staying in that yard for a time. That first day started before the sun was even up. We were all given a small first breakfast while the yard bustled with activity. There were all the sounds of a busy yard in the morning: clanking buckets, horses calling, stable doors opening and closing. A fresh, chilly pre-dawn breeze, mixed with the warmth of horses and stables.

The first lot of horses to go out to the exercise tracks were all the experienced older horses in full work, those who were preparing to race. First thing in the morning was when the sand tracks were freshly raked and at their best. It was the best time to do hard work, as the day was still cool and pleasant. Grooms vaulted up into the saddles, agile and light, and they all left the yard with a clatter of hooves and jovial chatter. Although the horses seemed calm as they disappeared into the dim morning, I could feel their energy and anticipation. They were noble and magnificent! When they finally returned from work, the horses were led back into the yard, steaming and relaxed. They were given a good hose-down and put back into their stables once they were cool, dry and clean. With another flurry of activity, the second lot left for the tracks. They were mostly horses in full work and some that were recovering from hard work or a recent race. The third lot to go out were usually the babies and horses coming back into work, or those that were taking a break. That was when the tracks were quieter.

My groom was a young Xhosa man, Mthunzi; his name means 'shade'. All the grooms in that yard were Xhosa guys, natural horsemen, most of whom took great pride in their charges.

That first day, Mthunzi put his saddle onto the half-door and came up to me, bridle in hand, chatting the whole time to his buddy Pumesile, who was tacking up the horse next door.

Mthunzi worked automatically – sure and confident. A shadow darkened the doorway and a low gravelly voice spoke harshly at the two. I don't understand a lot of Xhosa, but from the tone of voice, I imagine they were being told to hurry up! Which they did.

All tacked up and ready to go, my mane and tail were hurriedly brushed out, my coat was given a quick wipe and my feet cleaned. I was led outside and Mthunzi, still chattering to his friend, jumped lightly up onto my back. We walked out of the yard and onto a sandy track, where we trotted along with long loopy reins. The two friends shouted out to others who were on their way back to their yards. I think the comments must have been rude, because they both laughed uproariously at the grumpy comebacks! They rode with such ease and confidence, almost nonchalantly, giving us the confidence to move forward freely.

Arriving in an area where there were other horses ringing, we joined in with the circling horses. Presently the trainer walked into the center with his assistant and a few riders. All of us newbies were sent for a 'hack canter' around the hacking track. That was great fun; we trotted off in a group to a sand track that ran all the way around the whole training center and set off at a slow, easy canter. It gave us a chance to relax and move at a steady pace. Mthunzi took me to the front of the line as he soon found that my long stride needed more space. He held my reins lightly and that allowed me to stretch my neck, lower my head and use my hind quarters to work in the heavy sand.

When we happy hackers returned to the ring, we stopped near a vehicle that was parked next to a railing. Riders hopped off their sweating mounts and quickly undid the girths and removed the saddles. Mthunzi put my halter over my bridle and led me to a deep, inviting-looking sand pit.

I could see that other horses had rolled there and suddenly I was very keen to get down in that warm sand pit and have a good roll. There was a great deal of whistling as the grooms circled their mounts on various soft patches of sand, encouraging them to get down and roll. Ahhh ...... that wonderful relaxing feeling of having a good roll when one is hot and sweated-up – glorious!

We were led back to the yard and given a refreshing hose-down. I noticed some horses standing with their front legs in big buckets of icy water to help cool joints and tendons. Others were having their legs dried and bandaged. A lot of effort was put in to make sure that the athletes of the yard had the very best care and attention.

By late morning, we were left to relax in clean stables to enjoy a late breakfast and munch contentedly on our hay. I came to appreciate that quiet part of the day after the business of the morning; it was a chance to lie down, or just stand and doze. Relaxation is essential for mental health as well as physical well-being. That is true for racehorses as much as for anyone.

In the early afternoon, the yard would come to life again. We were taken out for a walk or a trot, mostly ridden bareback.

We were groomed to perfection and our stables cleaned out again. Mornings and afternoons, the assistant trainers went around with a big box of medical supplies and checked every horse with a fine-tooth comb. They had some horses trot up and down to check for unsoundness, and they tended to any cuts and bruises. Everything we ate was monitored. The vet, the farrier and the equine physiotherapist were all daily visitors to this yard. The vibe was one of energy and purpose. There was a genuine love for horses and racing. I saw that many of the horses and their grooms had built up a strong bond.

I found myself looking forward to each day, calling Mthunzi when I saw him on the other side of the yard. He often sneaked extra lucerne into my net and on our way back after work, he allowed me to graze the fresh, green grass that grew on the edges of the tracks for a few minutes.

My life became a happy combination of routine and fun. In the mornings our work was varied; one day a long canter, the next shorter, fast work. Sometimes we were ridden to the nearby beach. The roar of the surf and the rushing, frothy water was scary at first. Once we got used to the feel of the icy water surging around our legs, it was awesome fun! We loved to paw and splash in the chilly sea, always followed by a roll in the deep, warm sand.

I was popular amongst the work riders, who loved my long, smooth stride. Even though some mornings I felt really good, and I danced and pranced, I could never bring myself to unseat my rider, no matter how playful I was feeling. Some of the other horses had a wicked sense of humor and let fly with a few jumps "just to make sure their riders were awake".

I became a favorite with the boss as well and would often enjoy a treat from his pocket as he passed by. I loved it when his young daughter would come in the afternoons to visit us – she always ran to my stable, stood up on tiptoe and stretched her little arms out to me. I would lower my great head and blow into her fine hair making her shout out in delight.

"Olly, Olly!" and she would place her chubby little hands on either side of my face, and give me big, wet kisses on my nose.

I loved my life; I loved my work; I was keen to race, to earn my place..........

Chapter 5 – Champion Material

"When God wanted to create the horse,
He said to the south wind,
'I want to make a creature of you. Condense.'
And the wind condensed."

BEDOUIN SAYING

An explosion of reality crashes into my brain and spears my nerve-endings. I am back on that roadside, back in hell. There is a lot of activity. Strong arms lift me so that I am lying with my slashed legs folded under me. A rain blanket is draped over me, shielding me from the frigid rain. With great effort, I am able to lift my head and watch through swollen, bloodied eyes as the gray is carefully rolled onto a tarpaulin.

"Shouldn't you just put her out of her misery now?"

"No. I want to see how she is once we get her home. She does not deserve to die here after all she has been through."

Lying next to me, she is unrecognizable – gone is the fine, satin coat, and her once-beautiful head is now grotesque and swollen.

"Don't die!" I whisper to her. "Don't give those monsters the satisfaction."

Her ears twitch. I am sure she heard me; I am sure she understood.

People crowd around her and take hold of the tarp on which she now lies. The horsebox has been reversed as close as possible and the ramp is lowered. Bit by bit, the horse is maneuvered up into the horsebox. She struggles weakly, her pain must be excruciating. I feel relief when she is finally lying inside. Before the ramp is shut, I see the doctor treating her with various injections and medications while a helper places blankets as padding under her head and around her blood-soaked body. Finally, a warm, dry blanket is placed over her, and the ramp is lifted and bolted safely closed. With plenty of last-minute instructions and banging of doors, the horsebox eases forward and rumbles off down the road.

I am alone. I feel a bleak and desolate emptiness, and I call after her as the box disappears around a corner.

"How far is Zelda with the other box?"

"Five minutes away – she got caught up in the traffic."

A man approaches me with a bucket of fresh water and sets it down carefully in front of me. I dip my raw muzzle into the pure coolness, and I drink deeply.

"Not too much, young man," he says, and too soon he removes the bucket and places it to one side.

"I will give you more in a moment; too much water now will make you ill."

I feel a flood of warmth and at first, I am not sure what that complicated feeling is that is filling my heart. It feels like an age has passed since I have felt an ounce of kindness; an age has passed since I have heard care and concern in a voice. An age has passed since my life has mattered to anyone.

I had been in full work for a while. My coat gleamed and my muscles were hard and defined. I was working with the first lot now and was matched with older, more experienced horses. The physiotherapist worked on me often to keep me from injury. All of us youngsters were taken to the practice starting stalls to get used to the confinement and the noise of clanging gates. Initially the front and back gates were left open, and we were led through the narrow gap, then we were asked to stand inside with the gates still open. We worked for a while, learning to stand with the back gates shut, and then with both back and front gates shut. We were handled with great patience and kindness. The starting gates soon became old hat. Standing in the close confines of that narrow space along with the other horses was just a prelude to a glorious gallop on the grass track. We loved that; it was a good chance to test our wings. One morning the racing officials came to watch us and issued each of us a 'Starting Stall Certificate' – very cool. Now we could race!

The day I was waiting and working for, eventually dawned. Yesterday there had been a lot of fuss with trimming my mane and tail and cleaning out my ears. I had been bathed in the afternoon – with shampoo. On race morning, my mane was plaited and my coat groomed and polished. It felt very strange to have a plaited mane, but I must say, I felt particularly elegant. Mthunzi came into my stable; he too looked very 'jooshed up' that morning, wearing a jacket and pants that were not his normal, scruffy working attire. He put the bridle and halter on me, and a light cotton sheet with the stable name on it. He chatted and whistled as he worked. Presently I was led out of the yard and along the sand track.

We did not go to our normal ring, instead we down a back road to where horses from other yards were walking around. In front of a grassy bank stood a huge truck that had many doors along the side. The driver called out and started opening up the doors. One by one, horses were led into the narrow doorways and the heavy, metal doors clanged shut behind each one. Mthunzi led me up the grassy slope to one of the openings and I followed him straight into that confining space, without question. I heard the door close behind me and found myself standing in a compartment. All the horses in the truck stood side by side down the whole length, each one divided by a padded, rubberized partition. Our grooms stood at our heads. Mthunzi rubbed my forehead and stroked my neck. There was a lot of talking amongst the grooms, the horses stamped and snorted, the truck shuddered to life, and we were off.

My first race day! I will always remember it. Never had I seen such bright colors, nor seen so many people milling about. It was loud and vibrant. I was led into a stable to relax for a short time. The assistant trainer brought my racing bridle over – it was made of plastic and very light. All buckles, attachments and tabs were carefully taped and covered to prevent them from getting hooked up during the race. I was given a final wipe-down; my feet were blackened with polish and my face and eyes were wiped with a soft cloth. I was led to a walk way and circled with the other runners of the race. When my trainer came over with a tiny saddle on his arm, he was wearing a tie and jacket – I hardly recognized him. We went into a stall where the trainer put my saddle on me. The girth and surcingle had to be tight; a loose girth is very dangerous when you are racing. Everything was checked and double-checked; straightened and straightened again. My front legs were picked up and stretched forward one at a time to make sure nothing was pinching. The assistant rinsed my mouth out with a squirty bottle filled with water, and we were set to go.

Next was the parade ring. It was shaded by big trees and groups of well-dressed people stood on the manicured lawn in the center. There was a crowd of people leaning up against the railings that edged the parade ring. Presently the jockeys all came out wearing brightly colored shirts, with matching caps fitted over their helmets. They walked over to their respective trainers, expertly twirling their sticks. The jockeys shook hands with the owners, and the trainers gave them last-minute instructions. A bell sounded and we all turned in onto the grass. The trainer approached with a jockey at his side. I recognized him – it was Ron, the young rider who often took me out on the gallops. I liked him; he rode well.

"We are just going to give him this one race," the trainer said.

"Then he must take a break on the farm until spring. Keep him out of trouble, don't let him over-do it; you know how he loves to work." The boss legged the jockey up lightly onto my back.

Mthunzi led me out onto the big, grass track and I pranced, arching my neck as we joined the line of jogging horses. One by one the horses were turned around and their grooms released them. One by one we cantered (some of us quietly, some not so quiet!) down past the grandstands and on to the starting gates in the distance. My rider held me straight and steady with reins that were short enough to give me guidance and confidence. I understood what he wanted; we had practiced many times. Somehow, though, at the races one is filled with adrenaline and energy. It is very hard to stay calm.

I was slowed to a trot and then to a walk as we approached the starting stalls. There was shouting and calling from the officials and handlers who were busy around the stalls. The noisy crowd could not be heard from here, just the sound of people and horses preparing to race. There was the last-minute checking of girths, bridles and other bits of tack.

"Right big guy, no worries, let us have some fun." Ron patted my neck. A handler took me by the bridle and led us up to the starting gates. I could feel my rider shift in the saddle as he bent down and made sure his feet were secure in the stirrups. We faced up to the pens. Some horses were already loaded up and they waited in their narrow cages, impatient to be set free to run. I was loaded in and heard the gates close behind me. More horses loaded up next to me, we stood like coiled springs, waiting to explode. I stared through the wire mesh of the gates at the green of the track before me. There was a tense energy; I could feel my heart beating loudly in my ears. With a deafening clang, the gates sprang open, and I found myself running before I knew what was happening.

Being in an actual race was like nothing I had experienced before. The pace was hot and furious. It was serious competition. No messing around; no Mister Nice Guy! Ron was a confident rider; he promptly took us to a handy position, and we cruised just behind the leaders. I settled into a good gallop. The whole field were closely bunched as we covered the first hundred meters in a thundering battle charge. I heard nothing but the steady rhythm of horses blowing as they ran, the wind whistling in my ears and the occasional word of encouragement. I looked to the one running alongside me, I saw the fire of challenge as he eyed me back in return. We swept into the final stretch and the pace quickened. Energy and excitement exploded through the group of horses and riders. I lengthened my stride, reaching and stretching as I accelerated. My jockey changed his hold on the reins then he asked me to fly!

Whooooo!!!!! What a rush! What an awesome, exhilarating feeling to be allowed to run with no speed limit. Then I was brought back to earth, and we slowed to a trot. There was much praise. Talking excitedly, my rider turned me around and we cantered back to the noisy crowd. There was Mthunzi waiting for us, looking up at me with a beaming face. Smiling and rubbing my neck, he led me back into the parade ring and into the winners' enclosure. Everyone was smiling, talking, and patting me. I was jogging and prancing, still riding high on a wave of excitement and adrenaline. Ron dismounted nimbly and immediately undid the tight girths and removed the saddle. There was the flash of cameras as everyone posed for photos and then we were all ushered out so that the next race proceedings could begin.

Back in the relative quiet of the racecourse stables, I was given a wonderful hose-down, the fresh water sluicing the lathered sweat off my hot skin in foaming rivers. Using a plastic scraper, Mthunzi scraped off the excess water from my coat and I was then walked calmly around until I was feeling cool and dry. I was allowed only the occasional sip of water, even though I would have loved to gulp it all down.

"Not too much, my friend," I was told. *"You don't want to get sick."*

A searing pain slams me back to reality. The rain is falling steadily in icy sheets. I am still lying in the bloody mud.

"We need to get this horse out of here as quickly as possible."

A new voice floats out of the murky gray of the morning. The second horsebox had finally arrived and had been backed up as close to me as was safe.

"Let us see if he can stand."

A halter is placed on my head and people gather around me. I hear the encouragement in the voices, and I feel warm, reassuring arms trying to support me. I sit up and someone helps me to straighten my stiff front legs. I struggle for a short time, but I am beyond exhaustion, my slashed muscles as stiff as boards, my mind hovering on the brink of shutting down. I collapse, back onto that muddy road. The team of rescuers then carefully roll me onto a blanket, I feel shooting pain with every movement, and as I am maneuvered up the ramp and into the horsebox, I shake uncontrollably. My head and body are surrounded by the padding of dry blankets and a warm blanket is thrown over me. I feel the prick of a needle in my neck and a few minutes later my muscles have relaxed and the pain in my abused body recedes to a dull ache. I feel the presence of a person sitting quietly at my head. The ramp is lifted and secured, shutting out the driving rain, shutting out the dim light, shutting out hell. There is a vibration and rattling as we start to move. I am right on the edge of conscious thought, and the memories of the last time I was in one of these horseboxes. It was the beginning of a dark and desperate life.

Chapter 6 – The Beginning of the End

When something beautiful and fine is marked and worn down
Does that make it any less valuable?
No, indeed, the marks of living bring out its true beauty.

SHARLENE FRANCES

Yes, a dark and desperate life indeed. I would like to tell you that my trainer did all he could to keep me in his yard, that I was saved at the last minute by some heroic and magical turn of events. How wonderful that would have been! I do not know why I ended up here, or what twist of events occurred that my life suddenly took such a horrific path.

A few days after my race, a man I had never seen before came to my stable door with a halter. I stood quietly as he put it on and led me out through the front gate onto the road where there was a vehicle with a horsebox attached. The assistant trainer came out with us and stood by as the man led me up the ramp and tied me to a ring in the front. I heard the ramp shut behind me. I wondered where Mthunzi was. I expected to hear that familiar laughing voice any minute, and I waited for him to come through that little door in the front of the horsebox. Instead, all I heard were low solemn voices, followed by the shake and rattle of the horsebox as it pulled away. I called out; I heard no answering call. I was alone.

The journey was not very long and when I was backed down the ramp, I found myself at a training center in the middle of the city. I guessed there would be no break on the farm after all. A groom came and took me to the stable, yanking roughly on my lead rein. This treatment puzzled and worried me. Until now, I had always been in the hands of proper horsemasters and I had no reason to expect anything different.

The first thing I noticed about my new home was that the horses were lean and surly. There was no casual, friendly banter amongst the grooms and they treated the horses without thought or care. Of course, we were all fed good-quality feed and our stables were clean. We were groomed every day, and our routine care was to Jockey Club standards. That is where our care ended. We were not seen as flesh and blood creatures, just as a means to an end.

The type of work we did was very similar to what I was used to. We had the same type of tracks to work on, but here, I found myself struggling to keep up with the work that was demanded of me. My saddle pinched and hurt my back. My mouth felt bruised and sore from the worn bit and the rough hands of the groom who rode me. I no longer enjoyed my work.

One could say that the horses in this yard were badly-behaved and unruly, that their refusal to go onto the work tracks, the fly-jumping, the bucking and the 'sticking up' were due to stubbornness or that they were 'highly strung'. Mostly, their behavior stemmed from un-addressed pain issues that were either not picked up due to ignorance or were merely ignored and masked with painkillers. It is true that all yards have horses with issues – some worse than others. It is, of course, an unnatural life for any animal, no matter how well they are cared for. The difference between the good and the bad trainers, however, is in how the issues are addressed and the effort that is made to get to the root of the problems before they are compounded.

CHAPTER 7 – FLOGGING A DEAD HORSE

> "The horse does one of two things:
> He does what he does
> To escape life,
> Or, he does what he must
> To escape death.

SHARLENE FRANCES

I was at my new stables for only a few weeks when I was again on my way to the races. The pre-race preparation was similar to what I had experienced before, and I was washed, trimmed and cleaned. The next morning, I was led to that big truck with all the doors. We all loaded up. The grooms from the other yards were chatting and horses stamped and snorted as we pulled away.

At the racecourse we were taken to the stables at the back. I heard a familiar whistling and saw a figure walking across the yard with a bucket of water. My heart swelled with hope, and I called out. Mthunzi turned to me; he took a few steps in my direction but stopped short when another groom shouted out to him. His head bowed; his shoulders slumped. He turned and walked away.

Out in the parade ring, it was a similar scene to the one I remembered but somehow everything had changed. Colors were not as bright; the crowd was loud and overwhelming.

I felt stressed and anxious. The bell rang and the trainer, a small, wiry man, came up to me with the jockey and legged him up onto my back. I knew this jockey; he had worked me often. He had a hard face and even harder hands; I had learned that his stick was not just for show.

We joined in the line of horses and went out onto the track. As I was released, I turned to canter past the grandstand. My rider held me with reins that were too short; he had no give and I found myself pulling against the pressure. Behind the starting stalls, we circled around waiting to be called in for loading. There was a flurry of activity as last-minute checks were made. A handler came up, took hold of my bridle and faced me up to the narrow opening. I was led forward, the gate closed behind me. There was a tense pause as horses and riders waited, muscles bunched, ready to race. The gates slammed open. We leaped forward, straight into a fast gallop. I was immediately hooked in the mouth by a sharp jerk on the reins. I flung my head up in surprise and pain, then plunged forward again, but I had lost my stride, lost my rhythm and the other horses ran past me. I felt the sharp sting of the rider's stick and doubled my effort to get back into the race. I couldn't settle. My shortened reins would not allow me to lower my head and use my hindquarters to drive me forward. I felt pain shoot through my hollowed back and once again found myself pulling against that unrelenting pressure on my mouth. As we came into the final stretch of the race, I was already spent but I tried to accelerate with the rest of the field. I ploughed forward as my jockey brought out his stick again and struck me repeatedly on my sweating rump, with force and malice.

The feel of the rocking horsebox coming to a complete halt and the sudden silence bring me out of my rapidly darkening past and into a black present. Where am I? My heart is still hammering from the memories of a life that was on the edge. I feel restrained and panicked. I must stand! I must get up! I thrash and struggle as I try to stand up. The ramp is quickly lowered and light streams in.

"Sit on his neck, I don't want him to get more hurt than he already is." It is the voice of my special guardian angel. The Doc, my rescuer – she is here!

I feel weight on my neck, holding me down, stopping me from smashing my head against the side of the box. Calming voices and stroking hands help me to relax and take stock of my surroundings. I am no longer lying in the rain and mud. I am lying amongst dry blankets, listening to the sound of kindness, feeling the soothing stroke of gentle hands.

"Right! Let's get him out of this cold and into a stable" It's Doc's voice again. There is much discussion and maneuvering to get me out of the box and into the stable. Although I am just a skeleton-version of what I once was, I am still not that small, and I do weigh quite a bit.

At last, I find myself lying in a thick bed of clean shavings and straw. The base of the bedding is a decent layer of sand to prevent the cold from seeping through into my raw bones. I am propped up onto my sternum with my legs folded beneath me. I lift my head and am able to dip my nose into a bucket and drink long, deep swallows of cool water. A slice of fresh, sweet-smelling hay is placed within easy reach, which I gladly accept. Wow! I can't even remember the last time I tasted hay as sweet and clean as this.

"What a relief to see him eating and drinking; a most welcome sign, there is still some fight left."

Doc kneels next to me with a bucket of warm water and a bottle of wound-cleaning soap. Using wads of clean, soft cotton wool, she works steadily at cleaning me up. The clean water in her bucket very quickly changes to a deep red. Another bucket of clean water is set down and that too becomes dark with blood. She talks as she works. I soon tire and am allowed to lie stretched out on my side. The voice does not stop; the hands do not stop. After a while, others enter my stable and I am rolled over onto my other side. The cleaning of my physical wounds continues. They will heal much faster than those deep festering wounds that have shredded my spirit, that have pierced my soul.

We trailed in last. I was led back into the parade ring. There was no happy celebration, just excuses from the jockey as he took his saddle off me. He was called into an inquiry from the race officials, and I believe that he was suspended for excessive use of the whip. A small justice was done on my behalf, I guess.

I was raced again - more times than I could manage. Each race was worse than the one before. I hurt all over; my joints and knees ached and stiffened and the muscles in my back, quarters and shoulders were in spasm. The more I hurt, the harder I was made to work. I started to refuse to go onto the gallops and I learned to lean onto the bit to try and alleviate the pain. I became known as a 'puller' and 'very keen', and was promptly put into harder, more severe bits and over-tightened nosebands. The more the bits hurt, the more I tried to get away from the pain and the harsher my bits and tighter my noseband became. I found that my tight noseband was worse than the harshest bit in the world. It prevented me from swallowing or flexing my jaw and restricted my breathing. It was the worst torture ever invented for horses. Even an hour after my bridle had been removed, I still felt the harsh effects on my nose and jaw. I came to resent being handled and dreaded going out to work. I would fling my head up to try and prevent my bridle from being put on and made it very difficult for my noseband to be fastened. This only got me into more trouble – no matter how hard you try; the people will always win in the end; mostly by inflicting more pain than you started with.

Just a few months ago, I had looked forward to my work. I loved the people who worked with me; I was bright and attentive; I tried hard to do my very best. A few months that seemed like a lifetime. Now I stood with my head in the corner of the stable, not caring what was happening around me. Never in my wildest dreams did I ever imagine that my life would change so drastically. Never in my wildest dreams did I even think that people like these existed; that anyone could treat another living creature with so much disregard.

In my final race, I 'ran away' with the jockey on the way to the start. No amount of pulling on my hardened mouth could get me to slow down or stop. I was scratched from the race at the start, and the course vet declared me unsound. I had just turned three.

Chapter 8 – Hope and Choices

"Saving just one horse
will not change the world.
But surely it will change the world
For that one horse"

AUTHOR UNKNOWN

I am lying in the stable, unable to stand. People come in to roll me over every few hours throughout the day and night to prevent my muscles from atrophying. This happens when the muscles become starved of blood and oxygen due to lack of circulation; the muscle dies and there is no reversal. A vet has been called in to examine me and to do a police report.

"This is one of the worst cases I have seen," he says. "Have you found out who these horses are?"

"I have scanned them; they both still have their microchips. This is Hollers the Dodger, and the gray mare is Alaskan Sky. I haven't managed to locate their passports yet; we are still trying to trace the owners."

(Just after the foaling season, a team from the Jockey Club, consisting of vets and their assistants, go around to all the thoroughbred stud farms in the country. They microchip every foal, take blood for DNA testing and do the IDs for the passports. Every thoroughbred in the country is traceable – that is, if the microchips have not been cut out as in the case of some stolen horses.) The vet continues his examination.

"I think we should keep his legs bandaged for now; these injuries are going to leave bad scarring. His feet are worn down to nothing. It will be a while before he can put weight on them. The best we can do for these stab wounds is to keep them clean. Luckily most of them are not too deep – although some will need suturing."

The vet and my Doc work on me for what seems like hours. All four of my broken, ripped feet are wrapped in a special poultice to help draw out heat and infection. I am put onto a drip to help my system get rehydrated, given a painkiller and started on a course of antibiotics.

Mine is not the only life being fought for. I learn that in the stable next door, the gray mare – Alaskan Sky – is still alive. We are two battle-weary, wounded warriors fighting to stay alive. We must not give up. I hear her thrashing in the stable next door. I call to her and hope that she can hear me through the thick shadows of terror that must be crowding into her heart and soul just as they do mine.

"She must not give up!"

A voice from the other side of the wall echoes my thoughts.

"She must hang on just a little more. We need to give her something to hope for."

"Her emotional and mental trauma will be massive, much worse than her physical wounds. Both these horses have been through unspeakable cruelty. Poor Hollers, he had to have been starved and abused for some time before the race."

Again, I hear the thrashing of desperation; again, I call out to her.

"I have an idea!" Doc sounds excited.

The sound of muffled voices reaches my ears, and suddenly a bunch of people enter my stable. There is much banging of hammers and screeching as wooden planks are torn free from the nails that hold them together. Plank by wooden plank, the wall between the broken mare and myself is removed until there is no barrier. I struggle up from lying on my side, so that I can lift my head to see what is going on. These feelings of curiosity and concern – I thought they had been lost to me forever. I see a gray horse lying in a thick bed, much like mine. She too has been cleaned up, bandaged and treated. I remember her on that hellish night; those dead, glazed eyes devoid of any hope as she ran along next to me. Was she even then a 'dead horse running'?

I call out to her, but she does not raise her head; she does not even twitch. It is then that I realize a shattering truth.

As horses, we have only one choice that is open to us. We do not have the choice of what we drink or how much we drink, unless we are allowed it. We do not have a choice on what work we do, where we go or how we live. From the day we are born, our lives are governed and affected by the choices made by the people who own us and care for us. All we can do is respond to those choices. Even those born in the wild have no say on where they are allowed to roam or whether they get captured or not. The one choice that is left to us is simple: do we live, or do we die? For many of us, even that choice is taken from us without thought or concern. In circumstances where one is hanging on the precipice between life and death, only the will to live can get you off the edge. Only your will can make the difference between living and dying. For some, death is a welcome relief, and no amount of treatment or money can save them once they have made the choice. For others, the pull of life has strength; the instinct and desire to live comes with the hope that life is still worth the struggle. How strong in this little mare is the desire to live? I think of the brutality that she had endured in the past days, and I wonder if she could have anything left.

Chapter 9 – Diamonds in the Dust

"We are all broken; that's how the light gets in."

ERNEST HEMINGWAY

When I returned from the races, I was put into a small paddock that was more like a lunging arena. At first, I celebrated my freedom, contained as it was. I dropped down and rolled, leaped up and kicked up my heels and ran around bucking. It hurt a bit, but I felt joy at being allowed the freedom to move without constraint. It did not take me long to realize that I had in effect been abandoned. I no longer got groomed. When food was brought to me, it was only leavings, the feed that other horses had not eaten during the day. It was normally sour and dusty. My water bucket was often empty; it was never enough.

The day that Jake came, it was cold and rainy. I was standing hunched against the blasting wind, when a man entered the ring with a halter and rope in his hands. He walked with a stooped back and a slight limp. It was difficult to judge him; to know what to make of him. his face was lined, and he was quite thin. Black hair stuck out from under a knitted beanie that perched on the top of his head. He came and stood in the center of the ring with hands on hips and legs apart. He had a hard, weathered face, and he seemed to glower at me from under heavy brows. I stood across from this man and regarded him with suspicion. He put his hand into his coat pocket and pulled out a bunch of carrots. I pricked my ears up with interest. Carrots! Wow, it had been a really long time since I had tasted those! They had always been my favorite treat. I could smell the sweetness. The man called to me and whistled softly. Oh, my goodness, it was so very hard to resist the call of the carrots, and it was the carrot offering that eventually won me over. I walked up to him and carefully took the carrot from his hand. Munching and crunching happily, I stood as he put the halter on and checked me over. He slid a hand down each of my legs, clucking and muttering to himself. He ran his hand along my spine and hindquarters, shaking his head as I ducked away from the painful pressure. Lastly, he placed his hands on either side of my head and lifted it up so that we stood eye-to-eye. I looked into his dark brown eyes; there was something I could not place – an understanding, maybe? His face suddenly crumpled into a smile and his eyes sparkled.

"It seems to me that you are in the wrong place, my friend. You had better come home with me."

With that he turned and led me out of the ring, past the office where he collected my passport and release papers, then off, out through the gates and down the road we went.

The rain had stopped, and a watery sun started shining. I was allowed to stop along the way and graze for a few minutes whenever we came across a patch of green grass. As we walked down the road we stopped to chat to many friends, relatives and acquaintances. I got a lot of attention and more carrots – even apples!

The area through which we traveled was poverty-stricken and dilapidated. The houses that lined the narrow roads were small and many of them were in serious need of repair. They each had a little garden that was walled or fenced in some way. At first glance the area was sad and dirty; there was litter lying on the roadside, dogs, thin and gaunt trotted along the pavements searching for scraps, and children played in the muddy street.

As we continued, however, I noticed the children that were playing in the mud were laughing and shouting. Friends greeted one another with warm hugs and smiling faces. Mugs of soup and loaves of bread – scratched up from meager supplies – were offered to elderly people sitting on doorsteps. Most of the homes had clean windows and carefully swept walkways. I heard somewhere later that nobody had any plants in their gardens because they just got stolen straight out of the ground. Yet, despite such hardships, there was still a spirit of generosity, friendship and valued family relationships. Despite the threat of gang violence and intimidation, the harsh realities of drug and alcohol addictions and the rampant abuse of the vulnerable, there were still those who rose above such miseries, those who tried to lift others out of the mire.

It took a long time to finally reach the place that Jake called home; the sun was already sinking behind the rooftops and streetlights were starting to come on. Jake called out as he led me through a narrow garden gate. The door of the house before us flung open revealing the figures of a woman and three children. Standing on the top step, they were all talking at once.

"Oh, you got him!" said the woman.

"Beautiful, beautiful!"

Clapping her little hands, a small girl skipped and jumped down the stairs and as she neared us, she shyly held out a grubby palm. I stretched out my nose and blew onto her upturned face. She shouted out and giggled, putting her hands on either side of my face, she kissed me on the nose.

"No, no! He is not a girlie horse, Poppy." The boys, Joe and Danny, chorused together.

Much argument and discussion arose, with piping little voices putting forward the merits of me being either a 'girlie horse' or a 'boy horse'.

"Okay! That is enough; I am sure he will not mind being both. Let us take him to the back and make him feel at home, shall we?" said Jake.

I was led up the stairs and into the house. I had never been inside a person's house before. The kids lead the way, importantly marching ahead of us, through the lounge and then the kitchen and out through the back door into a small backyard. The yard was walled on all sides; the only way in or out was through the little house. I later learned that most of the horses in these areas were typically kept in this manner to prevent them from being stolen by gang members and other unsavory characters. Attached to the house was a wooden shelter that served as a stable. It was warm and dry, with a large bucket of fresh, clean water in one corner and a big pile of hay in another. The family all got busy making me comfortable. While everyone talked at once, I was brushed and cleaned. A bucket of feed was brought in and emptied into a manger at the back of the stable. Eventually, the half-door was bolted closed and secured with a padlock, then, with a chorus of goodnight wishes, the family disappeared into the house, leaving me to settle in for the night.

I felt the warm glow of security and peace. Some faith in humanity had been restored in me that day. For the first time in many months, I felt that my feet had touched solid ground, that I was no longer being swept along helplessly, to be swallowed up and forgotten.

Chapter 10 – The Good and the Very Worst

If you falter – they will catch you.
Look ahead!
Looking behind will still your pounding heart.
Looking behind will cause it to freeze with dread.
Plunge forward into the fray,
Keep Going!
Be brave son! Be brave!

SHARLENE FRANCES

The nights in such a place were far from peaceful. Loud music, dogs barking, gunshots, revving cars, shouting drunkards, police sirens, ambulance sirens and sometimes the wail of fire trucks rushing past, were all part of a normal evening. Later on, during that first night, Jake and his wife, Rose, came out to check on me. They found me lying down with their three children curled up alongside me. Shaking their heads, they carried the children back, amid sleepy protests, to their own beds. Upon their return, Jake and Rose made sure that I still had enough water, then leant up against my door for a while. Jake quietly smoked a pipe while I stood eating my hay.

"What are you going to do with him?" Rose asked.

"Let us get him sorted out so we can see what he is like," said Jake.

"*I am sure he never deserved to end up like this; that he has done nothing wrong. Too much greed and not enough sense – some people belong in jail!*"

After a few more minutes, they went back inside. Jake took great care to extinguish his pipe first.

In the days that followed, a whole new world opened up to me. While I was well cared for, I still had the constant anxiety that something ugly was waiting just around the corner. The circumstances were certainly not ideal; this was not the safest place for a horse – or any animal. Even the people were not safe. The power of fear and intimidation often seemed to outweigh the power of decency and kindness. People will go to heart-wrenching lengths to protect their families from the monsters.

I was in bad shape when I first arrived, but Jake had a lot of help from charitable organizations who made sure I was fitted with decent shoes and supplied with good-quality feed. Thoroughbreds are not easy to keep; we generally need more feed than other horses to keep us going, and we require a lot more care. Our feet and legs are not as tough, and we can easily go lame under the wrong conditions.

Surprisingly, there were a lot of horses in the area. Most of them were either Hackney ponies or a local mix-breed known by some as 'Westies'. These brave little horses came in all sorts of colors and were as tough as the people who owned them. The majority were hard-working horses and ponies that were used to pull carts around the city streets. These guys were mostly well cared for, as their owners knew the benefits of keeping their horses well-fed and sound – after all, how could they earn money with their carts if they had no one to pull them? A good cart horse was worth quite a lot of money and was very hard to replace. *Organizations such as the Cart Horse Society were instrumental in educating owners on proper horse care and making sure all the working horses were shod correctly as they spent all day trotting on hard and sometimes hazardous surfaces. The organizations helped out with veterinary care and advice and worked closely with the police and S.P.C.A who confiscated any horses that were abused. The owners were fined or jailed accordingly. Every working horse was issued with a registration number and the owners were held accountable for their horses.*

The cart horses in the city were tough and well-trained. It was not uncommon to see a pony and cart standing alone outside a shop, on the side of a busy street, patiently waiting for the owner to return. They worked all day, trotting along the roads with loads of scrap metal. Any over-loading, lameness or abuse would be quickly reported by the many well-meaning citizens who drove past in their cars.

This was not a life for sissies. Generally, the people who lived in these areas were very hard characters; abuse was rampant, and life was cheap. The horses were not molly-coddled; they were there to work - and work they did.

Jake was an upstanding man by the time I knew him, but he hadn't always been so. His childhood was one of neglect and abuse, and as a young man he had found it easy to be seduced by the gangs, by the idea of belonging somewhere, no matter what kinds of evil that involved. Then he came across a man who showed him that life could be different. This man had something that Jake had never known in his entire young life: hope. Jake saw that a family could be close-knit and take care of one another. Children were safe – whatever they might have to encounter in the outside world, they always had a place of warmth and security to return to. For the first time ever, he realized that a person did have choices. They could choose to stay in the dark, stinking bog, or to lift themselves out, to stand in the sun and breathe. Jake found that in order to lift himself up, he had to lift up others too. He cleaned up, found a job in the city and got married to his beautiful Rose.

The three kids were delighted to have me in their family. Every day I received a thorough brushing, with all three trying to outdo one another. Before Jake left for work in the city, he would clean out my stable and make sure I had enough food and water for the day. Although winter was approaching, the sun was still rising early enough for him to have time to take me out before he left for work. He would lead me back through the house and out through his front door where he would hop onto my back and the two of us would go for a quick jaunt around the neighborhood. He never used a bridle on me; I just needed the halter – we traveled light. We cantered along the grass verges and trotted along the sandy back roads. The early mornings were fresh and cool – and quiet! My back felt so much better, and my legs were no longer painful. Then it was back in through the house and into the back yard where we all enjoyed breakfast together. The kids liked to come out and eat their porridge while I ate my bowl of feed. I was allowed out in the small back yard during the day, and I had access to my stable if I wanted to go inside. When the children were home, they would all climb onto my back together and the three of them would sit there while I roamed around the back yard. Of course, there was always an argument as to who was going to be in front and the whole rigmarole of climbing up on boxes and stairs to get up onto my back, was something to see. There was always a lot of instruction and organizing from little Poppy as she supervised her two older brothers during the whole process.

I was so grateful that I ended up with Jake and his family. I was very well aware of how my life would have ended had he not come along.

There is the sound of a cell phone ringing and I realize once again that I am lying in the warm, dry stable. A group of people are getting ready to flip me over. They wait politely for Doc to finish her conversation on the phone.

"So, have the owners been traced?" There is a pause, then she speaks again.

"You have got to be kidding! No way! No wonder he looks like he does."

She nods and makes noises of agreement.

"So, did the police catch any of those bastards?"

I can hear the helpless rage in her voice. There is a silence as she listens to the garbled voice on the other end.

"How can anyone survive such a thing and still be sane? Man, that is so, so shocking…"

Now her voice is filled with profound sadness. In that instant I know what it is that she is being told. A deep, all-consuming grief overwhelms me and it rips my heart to shreds.

………. *Gang violence had been rife in our area for some time. We no longer went out in the mornings and the children had to stay inside for fear of stray bullets or worse. The whole area was in lockdown; you ventured out at your own peril. Jake was tense and strained and the children were quiet. They spoke in whispers and hardly ever laughed.*

"I need to get you all out of here to where you will be safe. I wish I had thought of this earlier, but I didn't think the situation would escalate like it has," Jake said to his wife.

"You should go and stay with your family – they live out of town."

"What about you?" she asked.

"I need to stay here, or our house will be ransacked, and we will be left destitute."

"Better to be alive – possessions can be replaced."

"I will not leave Hollers; you know what will happen to him."

Jake and Rose both stroked my neck. There were tears shining in her eyes.

"I wish there was a way we could take him with us."

They turned and disappeared into the house.

……….. The screams and gunshots were terribly loud. It was very late, but the night was alive with the sounds of violence and mayhem. Smoke came into my stable in thick billows, making it hard to breathe. I ran around my stable in panic. I looked over the door, snorting, my heart hammering in my chest. The back door was flung open, and a figure appeared in the doorway then stumbled up to my stable.

"We have got to get out of here now!" Jake came to me and put on the halter. Blood and tears streamed down his battered face and his raw, burned hands shook. He led me up to the back door. Smoke was thick in the house. I stood frozen on the threshold, unable to move.

"Come on Hollers!" he rasped. *"You will die if you stay here; we will both die!"*

He pulled desperately at the lead rope, I walked forward and followed him in. My early pre-race training allowed me to trust this man, to walk into a space where I would not normally venture. As we passed through the darkened house, I smelled the sharp scent of blood and fear. There were two shapes lying near the front door. I did not recognize these men; they lay very still, staring blankly up at nothing. I had never encountered anything dead before. I instinctively tried to keep my distance.

"Come, come! They cannot hurt you; they will not be hurting anyone now."

Jake spoke with an unusual bitterness. I wondered anxiously what had happened to the rest of the family.

The streets were now strangely quiet, but the occasional loud volley of shots shattered the silence. They were close. The wailing of police sirens sounded in the distance. The house a few doors down was on fire; nobody was trying to fight the fire; everyone was either in hiding or fleeing for safety. In other emergency situations a man could maybe jump onto the back of his steed and gallop off to safety. It was not so here: one had to be as small a target as possible. Jake doubled over into a crouch and, keeping to the shadows, he led me silently along the ghostly street.

The piercing scream of a woman came from the small shack just up ahead. Jake dropped my rope and ran flat out toward the sound. I stood where he'd left me, my head up, ears forward, nostrils flared, eyes bulging. All my senses were on high alert. I was held immobile by a heavy blanket of fear. I heard the sounds of a struggle, followed by gunshots – then *sudden, deathly silence. I was ready to run, but my feet seemed rooted to the spot. For what seemed like an eternity, I stood and waited on the verge of flight. Then the figure of a man lurched out of the shadowed doorway and stood swaying under the streetlight, and a loud mourning wail came from inside.*

I was so focused on what was happening ahead of me that I failed to notice a man approaching until it was too late. He had a hold of my rope before I had a chance to react. I backed away in fright and leaped forward, but he held me fast. With a jerk, he pulled on my head. He led me up to the figure that was still swaying under the streetlights. I did not want to go; I felt a strong sense of foreboding. As I passed by the doorway, I saw my friend Jake lying on the ground, covered in blood. His wife was kneeling next to his still body. Her clothing was torn, her hair was matted with blood and sand, and she was moaning in pain and grief. In the far corner the three children were huddled together, looking up at me with dirty, tear-streaked faces, wide-eyed and silent.

"Come on! The police will be here any second," shouted the man who clasped my rope.

"I must finish this lot off first. They need to be taught a lesson,"

the staggering man growled. He had a blood stain on the front of his shirt that was becoming larger by the second. He lurched forward, pointing his gun into the hut.

"I am gonna slaughter the lot of you!"

There was a click as he aimed his weapon, then he stumbled and fell face down, the gun skittering out of reach. The police sirens were getting louder. Panicking, my captor leaped onto my back, drove his heels into my ribs and slapped me with the lead rope. As I jumped forward into a startled gallop, I heard a shot. Rose was standing over the twitching body of her husband's killer, the gun in her hand still aimed at what used to be his head. I heard the frightened screaming of the children and as I plunged into the shadows, there was one last pleading, desperate cry:

    "Olly! Olly!"

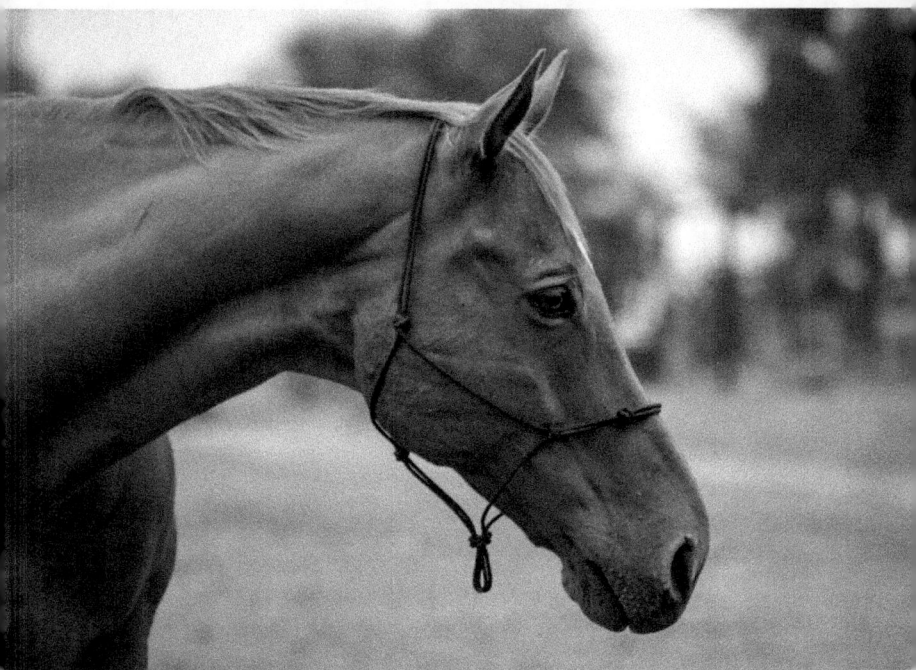

Chapter 11 – Bones in a Box

"Look back at our struggle for freedom,
trace our present day's strength to the source;
and you will find that man's pathway to glory
is strewn with the bones of the horse."

AUTHOR UNKNOWN

Like something one would find in a witch's cauldron, the days that followed were an ugly swirl of everything that was evil. A dark and oppressive shadow settled over my mind, I felt trapped in a nightmare with no hope of waking up, no hope of escape.

That terrible night, I was ridden hard down a maze of narrow, derelict streets and ended up in a bleak-looking neighborhood. By the time I was hauled to a halt, I was lathered up with sweat, my muscles trembled with exhaustion, and my sides heaved with the effort to breathe. I was bewildered and afraid, surrounded by strangers etched with crude, ominous tattoos, foul in both body and spirit.

'Sharps' was the name of the one that everyone answered to. I doubt anyone knew what his real name was; all the monsters went by nicknames. Sharps, of course, loved his knives; he carried an assortment on his person, and he was quick to use them. His sheer brutality and absolute absence of remorse were instrumental to his rise in the ranks. He was feared by everyone around him, with good reason.

As I stood with head hanging, the rider leaped off my back and went over to speak to Sharps, taking care to keep his eyes cast down.

"I found AK and Viper. They are both dead. They were in Jake's house. He must have killed them."

Sharps stared with dead, black eyes, his face a blank mask.

"Axel . . . he found Jake's wife and kids...... and killed Jake." The man kept his head bowed as he spoke. I could smell his fear from where I was standing, but he dared not show it and his voice came across clear and confident.

"Where is Axel now?" The question was deceptively casual.

"He is dead."

There was only the slightest hesitation.

"Have the family been dealt with?"

The voice again was casual, but I sensed an underlying tension and a violence.

"I did not see; the police came – I had to get away. This horse, it belonged to Jake."

"This was Jake's horse?"

The dead eyes shifted, and I felt their weight. The voice was malicious and chilling – the casual pretense had disappeared. The man sneered. He circled me, rubbing his hands – he seemed almost gleeful.

"Trust him to have a horse like this. Good for only one thing."

He turned to the man who had brought me.

"Put this horse into the box. I have plans for it."

With a sigh of relief, the man turned and took the lead rope.

"That was close. I nearly died," he muttered.

Yanking at me with the rope, he took me to a metal shed and led me into the narrow opening. It smelt of death. Before I could back out, I heard the heavy door slam shut behind me.

My prison was dark and stifling. There was just the odd rusted hole through which light shone in tiny dots. That was the only way that I knew it was daytime. There was no space to turn, nowhere to lie down, no food, no water, no air. On occasion I could hear voices outside and the tramping of feet nearby. Nobody came to open the door. I was left alone, tormented by memories, thirst and hunger. I had no idea how much time had passed since that unspeakable night. It felt like years. It felt like seconds.

The sound of voices just outside the box awoke me out of a stupor. There was a rattle as the door was dragged open, and light and fresh air flooded into the tiny space. I could not see directly behind me, and the narrowness of the space in which I stood did not allow me to turn my head. I backed out as fast as I could, before whoever it was behind me could close that door. I still had on the halter that Jake had put on me, and someone grabbed the swinging lead rope.

I found myself surrounded by monsters. Sharps was there. One of the monsters came forward with a bridle and grabbed my head. He jammed the bit into my mouth. It tasted of blood.

"This came along just in time for the Big Race," said Sharps. "Thanks to Jake!"

His laughter was a cruel and chilling sound. The other monsters laughed, and I felt a surge of fear and panic.

"Those others we got for this race lasted just a few days. We must make sure that this one makes it to the race."

Sharps turned and spoke to a person nearby.

"Cole! That is your job. If this horse dies before the race, you die with him."

The monster who had brought me to this place stepped forward and dipped his head.

Sharps slung the reins over my head and leaped onto my back. In one hand he had a long whip that he brought down on my flanks with force. I leaped forward and galloped down the road. The monster clung to my back like some vile predator. I could not outrun him; I did not have the strength to get him off. He lashed me with the whip with every stride. I was running blind. When he finally dragged me to a halt, I found myself back amongst the other monsters. I stood with my head hanging with exhaustion, blood and sweat streaming down my legs and dripping from my heaving flanks. There was a roaring in my ears. My shoes had been ripped off and my hooves were broken and split. I was not aware of being led back into the box until the slamming of the door sounded behind me.

A long time later, I heard the clanging of a bucket outside. By the light coming in through those little holes, I could tell it was still daytime. The door opened a crack and a shadow entered in behind me. There was barely enough space for the man – it must have been Cole – to move along the side of the box to my head. He set the bucket down at my feet then immediately disappeared back out. I lowered my head and drank. Within seconds, I was slurping the last of the water from the bottom of the bucket. My thirst still raged; I was beyond hunger.

I lost track of time as day and night blended together. Each day Cole brought me water. He took me out of that stinking box for a few minutes and let me pick on whatever grass I could find along the edges of the road. The bright daylight hurt my eyes and made them water. Cole seemed like an empty shell; he was an expert at hiding his thoughts. He never showed emotion. The brown skin on both his arms was tattooed with black wings spread in flight. He was always alone; he never spoke to me; he was neither cruel nor kind. I guess he did not want me to die just yet. Then he stopped coming.

How long I was left in that darkness I have no idea. When the door finally opened wide, I had to be pushed out. My legs were stiff and puffy. My once fine, gleaming coat was rough and matted with dried sweat and blood. My once strong, well-defined muscles were wasted away to nothing; the only things that showed under my dull, staring coat were well-defined ribs and jutting hip bones.

"This guy looks fast asleep! Get the horse ready. Maybe tonight we get to win the big money!"

Chapter 12 – The Devil's Day at the Races

"Let a horse whisper in your ear
And breathe on your heart.
You will never regret it."

AUTHOR UNKNOWN

"I think we should see if he can stand up today."

The voice of the Doc breaks through my thoughts and I feel a profound relief to be brought back from the clutches of those crowding memories.

"The sooner he stands up, the quicker he will heal."

There is a general nodding and buzzing of agreement as a group of people gather around me. With encouraging sounds and gentle pushing, they get me to sit up. They straighten my front legs out in front of me and everyone heaves together.

Horses stand up front end first, then back end. Cows are the other way around; they stand up with their back legs first, followed by the front legs. With my front legs holding me up in front, all I have to do now is lean forward and thrust my hind quarters up with my back legs. There is much encouragement and support from those surrounding me as I try to heave up onto my feet. My hind legs shake with the exertion and give way. I sit back down.

"Come, big horse, let's try one more time!"

Again, with renewed effort, everybody puts in everything they have. They want me to live. With all the willpower that I have, I strain to stand. There is a lot of excited chatter and celebration when I eventually find myself standing up on my own four feet. My four very sore feet. I don't mind the pain; it reminds me that I am alive. I have survived the monsters. I am not going to let them triumph. There is much fuss, patting, stroking and ruffling of my forelock. Everyone is beaming with pride and happiness. I am offered a carrot which of course I gladly accept.

"Awesome work! Well done, guys. We have gotten over a big hurdle – it should get much easier from now on for this boy. Now that he is up, I think we should close the partition between him and the gray horse – just halfway so that they can still see each other."

From the day that the barrier was removed, a great effort has been made to give the mare every reason to live. The knowledge that she was no longer alone to be engulfed by the horrors of the past allowed a small light to stream into her battered soul, and that gave her a reason to fight to the surface and breathe. She reached the point where she was no longer lying flat on her side but rather up, with legs folded under her, making it easier for her to eat and drink. She became interested in her surroundings and started to participate in life once more.

Now, it is evening and I stand dozing with my head over the partition. My night sounds have changed from the mind-battering noise of the city to the healing resonance of the countryside. I have come to enjoy the chirrrr-rruping of the big family of guinea fowl settling in for the night (which apparently takes a lot of organization and discussion), the harmonizing frogs, the melodic whistling of the nightjar and the soft whooo of the eagle owls conversing from the treetops. There is the occasional barking of the neighboring dogs. The mare is lying flat on her side, when she suddenly raises her head and looks at me. She strikes her front legs forward and with an almighty effort, she heaves herself up onto her feet. She stands for a few seconds on shaking legs, like a new-born foal. I call softly to her and there are echoing calls from the other horses in the adjoining stables. It does not take long for a person to pop their head over the stable door to see what is going on. Just as suddenly the head disappears and almost immediately there are a few more heads popping up to look over the stable door.

"Unbelievable! What an amazing day this has been."

Once more there is much celebration and fuss. Gray Mare (the name has stuck) is showered with praise, there is a lot of patting and stroking, and her stable fills with the delightful sounds of happiness and laughter. After a while, the angels that have been watching over the two of us night and day for what seems like forever, leave in twos and threes, still chatting animatedly. They had of course first checked on all of us, making sure we all had enough water for the night before heading for a well-earned sleep; the first full night's sleep since rescuing us from the clutches of hell.

Only Doc remains behind. I know that she loves the quiet contentment of being amongst her horses at the end of the day. There is something restful and soul-soothing about the sound of horses settling in for the night. The sounds of horses enjoying their hay; the soft blowing through velvet nostrils; the warm, sweet scent of fresh hay and clean shavings. Doc comes down the line of stables, spending time with each horse. I am waiting for her. I look over the half-door of the stable and watch as she approaches. She is finally here. I put my muzzle against her neck, she strokes my nose and scratches me behind my ears. I check her pockets knowing that she will have something there just for me. I am not disappointed. A piece of crunchy carrot, my favorite. During those dark days when I first arrived, she had slept right next to me, and if she could not be there herself, she always made sure that there was someone, so that I was never left alone with the demons that plagued my dreams.

"and I looked, and behold a pale horse:
and his name that sat on him was death,
and hell followed with him......."

REVELATION 6:8

Preparation for the races in this case did not mean the same thing as it did in the racing yards. I was taken to a hosepipe and washed down. The only reason they did this was that the monster who was going to ride me did not want his legs and pants to get full of dirt. They gave me more water than usual, noticing that I was ready to drop from thirst. (Couldn't have that before the race started.) The sudden access to so much water made me feel ill; it sloshed around in my empty stomach and pretty soon I was suffering from sharp pangs in my belly.

I longed to lie down, but as soon as my legs buckled beneath me, I was jerked up, and I received more than one hefty kick in the gut. My tail was cut as close to the tail bone as possible, and my mane was hacked right off. This, I learned, was so that the riders of the other horses couldn't grab you by the mane or tail and pull you off your feet during the race.

Like dogfighting, urban horse racing is against the law because of the immense cruelty involved. There are no rules, anything goes, the winner takes all. The prize is a substantial amount of money. Like anything monstrous, this is organized by the gangsters, the time and location are top secret and officials are kept silent by means of bribes and intimidation.

The big race is held once a year, usually on Good Friday, ahead of the Easter weekend. Horses are brought into the area for the race during the preceding month. These horses have either been given away or bought cheaply from unscrupulous owners. Many are stolen.

There are two types of illegal racing. One is Bush Racing. In Bush Racing there are some rules: no thoroughbreds; no saddles; all bits and bridles are checked prior to the race. Only straight dirt roads are allowed to be used as racetracks. The horses are looked after, because the horse needs to be able to earn money for the owner. These races are normally held out of town and are quite regular. The good bush racers are never used in urban racing, because even if the horse survives the trauma, they are never the same again and are therefore wasted. It is the 'reject' bush racers that end up in the streets on Good Friday.

In Urban Racing there are no rules. Heats are run during the day, and the final is run sometime during the night. The horses that place in the first heat, go up against the horses in the next heat, which means that some horses end up running in four or more grueling races during the day. The horses are run flat-out along paved streets and around sharp, uneven corners, where they often come down at speed. Monsters between the ages of eight to ten are the riders. They stick on anything, and winning is their only goal. They do not care about the horse they are riding, as long as they can pass the finish first. They have been 'pressed' into service by the gangs and are out to prove their worth. The prestige and reward for winning the race is huge. Long whips and knives are commonly used to get maximum speed and a greater advantage. The riders will attack one another and their opponents' horses as well as their own mounts if it will get them ahead.

I cannot describe in detail the scene at the Good Friday races; that will surely drive me to the edge of insanity. It is a scene that comes from hell itself. All I have is a blur of sights, sounds and smells. It is a blur of screaming, terrified horses mixed with the frenzied roar of the monsters. A mix of wild, rolling eyes, the cracking of whips and the panicked clatter of hooves on the tarmac. There is an overwhelming fear that clutches and squeezes your heart. There is the acrid smell of sheer terror mixed with sweat, blood and dust.

I had a monster on my back. This monster worked for Sharps. It carried knives. I found myself lined up with other horses. Some were standing, wide-eyed, feet planted in the ground, shaking uncontrollably. Gray Mare was there, rearing up in fright and confusion. The loud crack of a gun had everyone leaping forward. My world narrowed down to the *cracking of whips upon sweated, bloodied flanks, the shouts and curses, the desperate drumming of hooves, the frantic blowing of horses straining to escape from the monsters that clung to their backs. Fear surged through my starved muscles and gave me the strength to keep up with the other runners. Horses came down at the first corner, stumbling on the uneven surface, slipping on the gravel edges. I managed to avoid the mangle of horses and monsters. I dared not look. We careened down the next street as if the devil himself was at our heels – the devil was certainly there that day, along with all his demons. They danced amidst the flying whips and flashing knives; they laughed as the blood and sweat flew into my face as I ran. My mind was close to shutting down and I looked into the eye of the one running alongside me.......*

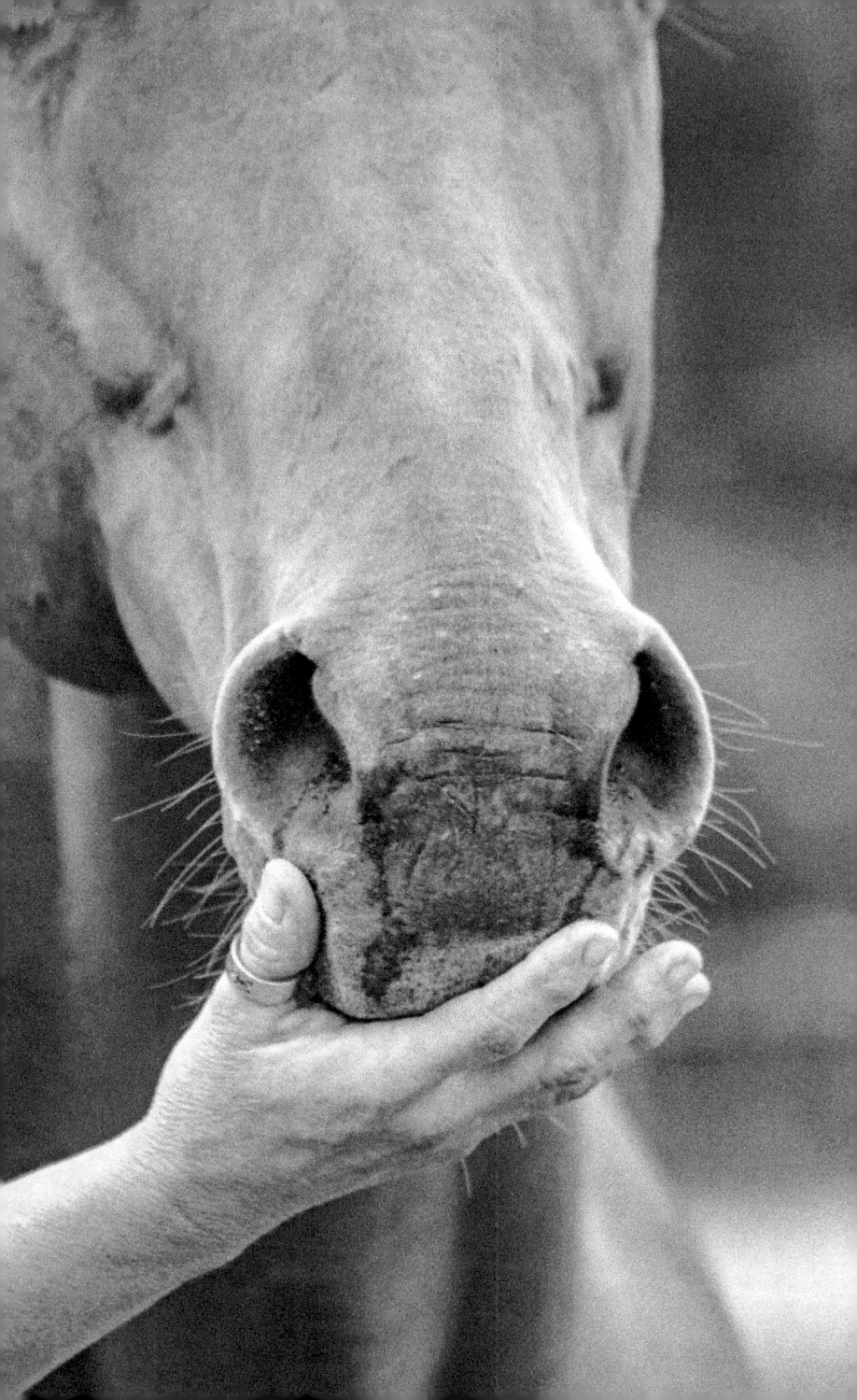

Chapter 13 – The Angels' Revenge

"Now I saw heaven opened,
and behold, a white horse
and he who sat on him was called
Faithful and True."

REVELATIONS 19:11

The rooster wakes up very early and starts his crowing before the sun is even up. There is of course a lot of chirping and chittering from the large family of guinea fowl as they begin getting organized for the day. As soon as the sun peeps over the hills, we all start looking for our breakfast – even though we know that it is still an hour to go before there will be any movement in the direction of the feed room.

At the sound of the feed room door opening, there is a chorus of neighs, whinnies and brays (from the donkey tribe), and eager heads pop over the stable doors. Most of us in this yard have known what it is like to go without food; we have felt the neglect and cruelty of people. Most of us arrived here in pieces, broken in body and spirit. We all have our own stories, some worse than others, all of them heart-wrenching.

After breakfast everyone is taken out and put into their paddocks. Gray Mare and I are usually left in our stables as our feet cannot take weight for extended periods of time, and we both spend large parts of the day lying down to ease our feet, legs and aching muscles.

Today, though, we are not left in our stables. Doc comes to my door with a halter, chatting to her son, Victor, who is with the gray next door. Victor was another of the angels who helped us get through the blackness. Now, Doc opens my door and slowly leads me out of the stable. It has been a few weeks since I have been able to get out. The past weeks have been a mix of the darkest of nightmares and a bright wash of hope. Doc allows me to move at my own pace, which is slow. Although I have poultices bandaged to my feet that provide some cushioning, the paving in front of the stables pushes into my bruised soles. We make it to a large square of thick green grass; it is springy and giving. That feels much better. We stop to rest. I see the gray, with Victor, progress slowly over the cement and onto the lawn. We both immediately lower our heads and start to graze on the sweet, green grass. Doc and Victor hold our lead ropes loosely, letting us move about at will to enjoy the fresh grass and golden sunshine.

"The police phoned; they have managed to locate the owner of Alaskan Sky," says Doc.

"Really? Who is it?"

"They didn't say. I need to go the station today to file my side of the report, so I will get more details there. She is not stolen. We are definitely going to press charges for animal abuse."

"What about Hollers? Any news there?" asks Victor.

"That is a different story. He was stolen – the police are still trying to trace his owners. They may be in hiding;

there is some gang issue with the family that owned him. The father, who used to be part of the gangs, was found murdered just before the Good Friday races – they must have been out to get him. The rest of the family have disappeared. Maybe I will get more info later on."

The last images I have of that little family are imprinted onto my brain. The fear and sorrow I saw in their eyes that dreadful night, remain heavy on my heart. I do not know what happened to them. I want to believe that they are safe.

We are out on the grass for just a short period of time before we are put back into our stables to relax for the rest of the day. In the afternoon, just before feed time, we are again taken out onto the grass for a short walk-about and a graze. The discussion turns to the happenings of the day and the progress that was made at the police station.

"I got the passports of both the horses," Doc says.

"Alaskan Sky has amazing breeding; she is twelve years old. I checked her racing form; she was a real champion. Either won or was placed in every race – earned her owners a large amount of money. She went to stud, was a broodmare for a number of years. Her foals have all been in the money. When the stud farm sold up, she was sold to an idiot woman called Gretta who only had the mare for six months before she tried to sell her on. This woman, Gretta, initially asked for a lot of money, thousands, but ended up selling her for a mere five hundred to the guy who collects her rubbish. That woman should be in jail! He obviously bought the mare for the Good Friday races. I guess it is a good thing that she wasn't in that area for very long; poor girl, those few days that she was there must have been a total nightmare."

"So, can anything be done to this Gretta who sold the horse without care in the first place?"

Victor sounds cross and frustrated.

I look over to where the gray mare is peacefully grazing. She had lost a lot of condition in those first few weeks following the race, but now she is starting to pick up nicely. Her scarred coat is mending and the slash on her throat is now just a thick pink line. The sutures have already been removed. Her fine, milk-colored mane is starting to grow, but her eyes have not yet lost that haunted look of one that has been abused to the brink of death. That will take longer than a few weeks.

"People need to be more responsible about their animals. One cannot just get rid of them to the first person that comes along. There are often very bad consequences for the animal in such cases, and none for the owner. The owner carries on blissfully unaware and uninterested in what becomes of the animal they have so casually discarded," says Doc.

"We can, however, prosecute the guy who owns her now. He will have to sign the mare over to us. He has a lot to answer for. The police already have him in their custody. Hopefully he spills the beans on other people that are involved, although we cannot count on that."

"So, when is the court date set for?" Victor asks.

"We go next week to testify," Doc says.

"Any more news on Hollers?"

Doc is standing next to me. She strokes my shoulder, assisting me with flicking pesky flies off my sides where my very short tail can't reach.

"Still not much, his passport was found in the house. The family's neighbors are watching the place while they are away. There is still no word as to where they are. Hollers is just a youngster; he will be turning four in October. So much has happened to him in his short life. I checked his racing record; it looks like he was raced far too often. Bloody ignorant trainers. His owner must have been a dumbass of note! It is about time that racehorse owners take responsibility for their horses' lives. It is far too easy for owners to offload horses when they no longer want them."

We are led back into our stables for feed time. There is the usual end-of-the-day activity as hay and water buckets are topped up, follow-up medications are administered, and fresh bandages and poultices applied. Dinner is served eventually amid the usual chorus of hungry horses and donkeys. Finally, when everyone is settled and eating, a special quiet descends. There is a perfect peace around horses as evening settles that can only ever be experienced by one who allows that gentle sweetness and pure contentment to flood into heart and mind.

"for the Angel of Death spread his wings on the blast,
And breathed in the face of the foe as he passed;
And the eyes of the sleepers waxed deadly and chill,
And their hearts but once heaved,
And forever grew still!"

LORD BYRON

It is just past midnight when a commotion outside the stables startles us into wakefulness. We all rush to our doors to look out and see what is happening, momentarily blinded as the lights of a vehicle flood into the stable yard. Some horses call to one another with a need for reassurance at the sudden disturbance. The engines are cut and there is the sound of the horsebox ramp being lowered. Voices reach us, urgent and strained.

"Come! We need to get this horse into the stable straight away!"

The stable lights are switched on. There is much discussion and maneuvering along with the sound of hooves banging against the metal sides of the horsebox. A group of people slowly emerge from the shadows of the horsebox with a horse lying on a blanket between them, and they carefully get it into the stable next door to me. Looking through the metal mesh window that is set into the partition wall on the other side of my stable, I see people bent over the shape of a little bay horse lying in the bedding and I hear the concerned and soothing whispers. My heart is filled with grief. Another victim. Another innocent soul, so broken that it does not even have the strength to stand.

The team of angels work methodically. Sadly, they have all become experienced at handling this kind of situation. Sadly, they have had to pull horses out of hell so many times that they can follow the procedures without direction or second thought. The large medical box is brought into the stable. Buckets of warm water are brought, and the vicious-looking wounds are cleaned and attended to from head to tail. A drip is expertly set up. The angels work quickly and quietly, making sure not to frighten and stress the horse any more than he already is. Soon they have their patient as comfortable as they can manage. They try to get the horse to drink, but he is too weak to lift his head. Fresh, clean water is squeezed into his dry mouth using a sponge, carefully so as not to allow the water to get into his lungs.

"This is all we can do for this poor chap for now. I'll stay and watch over him, you guys will have to come back later and help to turn him. It is nearly 2am already; he can settle and rest now. You all can do the same. If this little man survives the night, we have a lot of work ahead of us to try and pull him through."

Doc sounds sad and tired.

A blanket is put over the little horse and preparations are made for the remainder of the night. Zelda brings a flask of coffee. I remember Zelda from when I was taken off the roadside and brought to this sanctuary of healing; she drove me here. The two friends speak softly as they share the flask of coffee, sitting on the bedding alongside their patient, stroking his neck and rubbing his head.

"Phew! What an evening," says Doc. "Do you know who it was that tipped off the police?"

"No, what a mess. The guy sure had it coming by the sounds of it – yup, payback is a bitch!"

During the night, from the quiet discussions going on among the different people who come in to aid Doc, I manage to piece together the whole story:

It was in the evening, after everyone had settled in for the night, that Doc received a phone call from the police.

There was a horse trapped and in severe distress; please could she come and assist. The police had had a tip-off earlier about gang activity in the area and hits that were planned for certain individuals. When they arrived on the scene, they found the body of a man lying in the door-way of a narrow, metal box. He was lying face down in a heap of stinking horse manure that had been left to pile up for some days. There was a horse trapped inside the narrow box; it had gone down and was unable to stand. It was badly wounded and traumatized. When the dead man was rolled over onto his back, the police found that part of his face was caved in. Knives were found on his person and a large dagger was found near the door. From the streams of blood that were oozing from the horse lying inside, they suspected that this monster had set about stabbing and torturing the horse while it was trapped in the narrow space. A hefty dou-ble-barrel kick in the face is probably what knocked this monster down. It did not explain, however, the fact that the knife man was lying face down in horse manure. It seemed he had been smothered in it; he had choked on it and suf-focated. Somebody had finished this monster off. The area was secured, and Doc was called in to take care of the horse. They had to break down the front of the box to gain access to the little horse and help him out.

The dead monster was identified as Sharps. He had taken great pleasure at inflicting pain on others. The mem-ory of his dead eyes and sneering face filled me with panic and terror, even now that I had learned of his sticky, well-deserved demise. His knives and his relentless whip had stained many lives like a blight. Humans and animals alike had suffered unimaginable pain and sometimes death for his own demonic enjoyment. I thought of what the last moments in this world must have been like for him: a foul blackness and excruciating pain……. the helplessness of being unable to do anything to prevent it from engulfing him forever. No amount of manipulation and power could change the fact that his life was ending with his crushed face smothered in a pile of stinking horse dung that, ironically, came from the hapless horses that had been in his clutches. As these thoughts and images cross my mind, my heart lifts and I feel wonderfully free.

Some days into the investigation, a police vehicle pulls into the yard in the late afternoon. The officers get out and come over to speak to Doc who is busy replacing the bandages on my legs.

"Hey Hollers!" They both greet me warmly.

"Unbelievable how he has recovered. It is good to see."

The officers stroke me on the neck as they stand speaking to Doc.

"How is the little horse from the other night doing? I believe he made it through."

"He is doing okay; he is not out of the woods yet – but we are hopeful."

The little guy is lying in the stable next door to me. He is managing to lift his head to drink water out of a bucket and has started eating hay. Food is being introduced slowly, with teff the first form of food offered. It is a fine, easy-to-digest hay. Teff and lucerne are a good start.

"We brought you something that you might find interesting. This was found inside that box where the horse was trapped."

Doc finishes the bandage and stands up to face the two policemen. One of them holds up a halter. It is cracked and crusted with dirt.

"Look at the name on the side," the policeman says.

"Hollers the Dodger," says Doc softly.

I recognize it as the halter that Jake made for me. His wife, Rose, had carefully sewed the letters of my name onto the side piece. The children had all put their decorations on it too. The boys scratched on a bolt of lightning and skull and crossbones (yeah sure: beware of dangerous Hollers! I always found that amusing). Little Poppy had asked her mother to sew on a shiny flower sticker and a red sparkling heart. As Doc stands holding and examining that halter now, I notice there are still bits of the red sparkling heart attached to the noseband.

"Hollers was in that box?"

She swallows hard. When she looks up, her eyes are flashing with anger.

"Hollers was in that box! That freaking good for nothing son of a bitch!" Those are not the exact words she says – I cannot repeat the exact words.

"There is something else," the cop says. "There are reports of the person who may have finished off Sharps. He has black wings tattooed on his arms – that is all we know so far. Seems that he has disappeared."

Black wings? I recall a man with black wings tattooed on his arms. I remember the emptiness and the careful detachment. Cole! When he stopped coming with water, I thought he was dead. Murdered by Sharps. I realize then that angels come in all forms; some even live among the monsters – one might even mistake them for a monster. Some angels live under the cover of the blackest of shadows. They are made to witness unspeakable acts; they wait for the opportunity to arise. Then they strike with an almighty vengeance!

The police vehicle disappears out of the gate and Doc leads me back into my stable. She stands for a long while staring at that halter in her hands, then turns, buries her face into my shoulder and cries for an hour.

Chapter 14 – Fun And Games

"Go out with your horse.
Leave your watch and the world behind.
Return with hearts refreshed,
And spirits soaring."

SHARLENE FRANCES

Many months have passed since we were left for dead on the side of that road. Alaskan Sky and I have flourished under the gentle care of Doc and her dedicated team of horse angels. We have both become strong and gained enough weight to pass as normal. Every day we are put into a large grassy paddock along with Little Chap, the bay horse that arrived the night that Sharps was killed. Chaps is not really that little; he was so skinny and terrified when he arrived, that he appeared a lot smaller than he actually is. The name stuck. Chaps is a spunky Arab/Westie-type – he loves to prove how fast he is. We let him win most of the time. He is an absolute hero in my eyes – a real badass!

One morning, Doc arrives at my stable with a saddle and bridle.

"Hey, my boy! How would you like to go for a fun jaunt around the farm?"

She tacks me up and leads me out into the yard. I see that Amber, one of the girls who sometimes helps out in the yard, has Alaskan Sky all tacked up and waiting to go. Neither of us is nervous nor anxious about being ridden again. We have complete confidence that we will not be hurt or find ourselves in trouble.

Doc leads me to a mounting block and swings lightly into the saddle. I stand politely as she adjusts the stirrups, re-checks the girth and gets comfortable. I have to admit that it does feel strange to have a saddle on again after so long. The gray mare prances along next to me; I can see that she too finds it kind of weird.

We are not taken very far, but the change from our usual routine makes the outing into an event. We follow a sandy path that leads through a stand of trees and then through a bushy, more wild area. The day is glorious. The sun is like liquid gold; everything is fresh. We trot along the path until we get to the fence, then we swing left and head for home. On the way, Doc spies a log that has fallen across the pathway, and she aims me straight at the obstruction. I wait for the signal to stop or turn; instead, she asks me to keep going. I feel her anticipation and delight as she aims me straight, we approach the fallen tree, and I hop over it as smooth as butter. She whoops with joy, and I break into a canter, kicking up my heels – I can't help it. Gray Mare was right behind us and pulls up alongside. We hear our riders laughing; they pat us on our necks and ruffle our manes. I look Gray Mare in the eye and see the sparkle of mischief and fun.

A person has fallen in love with Gray Mare - Alaskan Sky. Amber showers her with gifts, love and attention as often as she can. Gray Mare has come to look forward to seeing Amber and calls to her when she sees her coming across the yard. It is good to see the mare putting her trust into another being.

One morning Zelda arrives with the horsebox. Amber is with her, jumping around with excitement, her face shining with happiness. She has a brand-new halter in her hands and fairly dances up to Gray Mare's stable. The mare greets her friend as the girl enters the stable. There is much talking and singing coming from that side and I look over the partition to see what is happening.

"Don't worry, Hollers," says the girl. "I am taking this darling home with me, but you will still get to see each other sometimes, I am sure."

Amber comes over and rubs my forehead and kisses me on my nose.

"You are such a special guy; I wish I could take you too."

She turns and leads Gray Mare out of the stable to the lowered ramp of the horsebox. Doc is standing there with Zelda. The three ladies talk animatedly for a while. There is much fuss with loads of hugs and pats given to the mare as she stands happily among the laughing women. Presently it is time to go, and Alaskan Sky walks into the horsebox without a second look.

"Don't worry, my lovely girl, you have a friend waiting for you in your new home. He is a cheeky little pony, but I am sure you will sort him out."

The ramp is lifted to many comments and jokes about ponies and their legendary attitudes and who would be sorting who out. As the horsebox starts to roll off, I call out to my dear friend and an answering neigh comes back just before they disappear from sight.

I miss my friend; we have traveled a long, hard road together. Her vacated stable is not empty for long. Within a couple of days, the empty space is taken by a horse that is so sad and broken that he stands all day facing the far corner with hanging head and empty eyes.

It is very difficult to give any creature a reason to live when, from the day they were born, they have only ever known cruelty and abuse. The near-fatal injuries that this horse suffers are not physical. The challenge here is to lift him high enough out of the black depression and misery that engulf him, for him to see the sun and endless horizons.

The past month has been strange without Gray Mare around. The sad little black-and-white horse is put out in the grass paddock with me, Chaps and three other horses. He keeps to himself. He goes through the motions of life, but never actually partakes of it. At least he is eating, but everything seems to be on automatic. His name is Soldier Boy. This soldier certainly is suffering from Post-Traumatic Stress Disorder.

Little Chap is now known as Happy Chap – he is such a joker, always up to something crazy, and he is especially good at opening doors and gates. Everything must be padlocked and wired-up to prevent horses from escaping and wreaking havoc in the gardens and the rest of the farm. We all love it when Chaps manages to open the gate to the paddock.

I am not sure why, but there is a law that seems to apply to most of us horses – it goes as follows:

"If you are in a place that you are not allowed to be – then run! Have a party! Gallop around as much as you can, do not worry about the going, do not worry about wire or bits that might get stuck in your feet, have a blast! Go, go, go!"

It means mayhem and panic for people when horses abide by this law. It applies when a person falls off, when stable doors are left open or when a horse gets away from a person. The more horses running around, the more fun it is.

It is during such a time that little Soldier comes to life. The five of us are running around, bucking and kicking, doing 'fly-bys' at reckless speed. (Fly-bys are when horses trot very sweetly up to the person trying to catch them and then suddenly sprint past! If you add in a buck and a kick, be careful not to take that person out as you fly by). I hear a pathetic little neigh coming from the direction of the open paddock gate. There is Soldier Boy, standing with his gaunt head held high and his fuzzy ears pricked up. We all stop to watch as he trots forward, his scraggly tail up and his scrawny neck arched. Welcome to our world, lovely boy!

"Will you all please get back into the paddock now before I put you all into time out!"

It is a plaintive wail from the poor guy who has been trying to catch us for the last thirty minutes. We have no idea what 'Time Out' is, but we hear him all the same. We have all settled down now anyway, and I allow him to put a halter on and lead me back to the paddock. The others follow and we all, Soldier Boy included, continue with our grazing as soon as we hear the gate close behind us. There is a sound click as the lock snaps shut and the gate is wired-up for good measure.

Chapter 15 – Let's Go Jumping!

"Some days just are……
and some days are just giant!
Let's choose!"

SHARLENE FRANCES.

There is something different about this morning.
There seems to be a different buzz. The horsebox pulls into
the yard, and I wonder what is going on. I see Doc's jumping horse, Ben, is being prepared for loading, when my
door is opened, and Doc comes in with a halter.

"Hey Holls, we are off to a show. You can come for
the ride; the other fella will need some company."

A show? No idea……. maybe it is something like the
races? But I have done no training! There is certainly a lot
of brushing and cleaning going on. Doc leans out of my
door and shouts over to Victor.

"Take the spare saddle, it fits Hollers. That bridle is fine."

The ramp is lowered, and large nets filled with hay and
lucerne are fastened to the front of the box. The vehicle in
front is loaded up with feed, buckets, tack and an assortment
of boxes and bags. Finally, we are loaded into the horsebox
and the ramp is closed. With a rattle and a shake, we set off.
I wonder if we will be coming back, I call through the little

window and I hear a faint answer from Chaps. The other horse, unconcerned, is pulling at the hay in his net. I decide that all is okay. I know that Doc and Victor are in the towing vehicle, so everything should be fine.

We travel for what seems like an hour and finally we arrive at our destination. I back out down the ramp and look around with interest. There is a lot of hustle and bustle. Children are bombing around on ponies; there are horses of all shapes and sizes. We find a spot under a large tree next to an enclosed grassy area. Our nets are tied onto the rails and our buckets of water are placed close by. The grassy area has brightly-colored obstacles – like free-standing gates scattered around. I watch with astonishment as horse and rider go around the field jumping the colorful gates. Some go very fast; others do not want to go at all. The small ponies with their young riders' race around the course as if their lives depend on it.

"I think I am going to give Hollers a go over these jumps," says Doc.

What!? No! Really? I must admit, it does look like fun. Perhaps I will give it a shot.

Doc tacks me up, jumps up onto the saddle and takes me out to an area where there are horses going over practice jumps. She knows a lot of people, and after she chats to a lady standing at the gateway, we are allowed through. I am trotted around in circles and around the arena, really concentrating on our work when we hear a shout.

"Hey! There you are, been looking all over for you. Oh, awesome! You brought Hollers."

A girl comes trotting into the practice arena on a smart gray horse. The horse trots like she is floating, her fine neck gracefully arched. There is only one horse I know that looks like that! I skid to a halt, and I neigh very loudly. My heart is so filled with joy that I can hardly contain myself. I realize in time that Doc is still in the saddle. I jog over to my darling old friend, trying to be as sedate and cool as I can, which is a big fail - I am all but bouncing out of my skin. The two ladies are laughing as I reach my Gray Mare, my Alaskan Sky. We greet in the usual horsey way, with a lot of blowing and squealing. Once we have settled back down, Doc asks Amber if she can give us a lead over the practice jumps. Doc keeps me straight as we follow Amber and the gray. We pop over the small jump. It is not difficult; it is like jumping over the logs at home – except that these are colorful. I soon get the hang of it, and I am happily jumping without our lead. Doc is very pleased, and she makes a lot of fuss over me.

We are entered into the same two classes that Amber and Alaskan Sky are entered in. The course is designed for young horses and novices. The jumps are low, the track flows easily into each jump with plenty of space. We walk amongst the jumps when our turn comes. The voice on the loudspeaker mentions my name and a bell rings. Doc guides me around the course with expertise and confidence. I can tell that she is having a great time. Each jump is different, a different color and design, but none are challenging. There are ten jumps, and we complete the course with ease. Doc pats me and rubs my mane. We stand on the outside of the arena and watch as Amber takes Gray Mare around the course. They do not make any mistakes. Gray Mare listens carefully to what Amber is telling her, and they also go clear. We are called in along with other horses and riders to accept our Clear Round rosette and then we canter around the edge of the arena and out the gate.

For round two, the course is the same, and the jumps are the same, just a little higher than the first round. No worries for Doc and Hollers, and no worries for Amber and Alaskan Sky. We have got this and once again we are cantering around the edge of the arena with another Clear Round rosette fluttering on our bridles.

Doc is very happy, and I really enjoyed the jumping, a lot more than racing. My bridle and saddle are removed, and I am given a hose-down and then allowed to relax in the shade with a net of hay and a bucket of fresh water. Amber stays to watch the next rounds. Gray Mare stands next to me sharing my hay. A little later in the day we watch Doc ride Ben. I see that the jumps are much higher and wider, the track is tighter and a lot more challenging. The riders and horses in these events are focused and precise; these courses take practice, ability and a great deal of confidence. The Announcer uses a different name for Ben, he introduces him as 'Stoneyhurst Dogs of War'. Wow! I see Ben through new eyes as I watch the glorious way that he flies over the jumps with so much ease. He is no longer that grumpy old biddy that mooches around the paddock and looks at everyone with laid-back ears, as if they are just wasting his time. No, in that arena he is a whole different horse. He is proud and fairly exploding with energy. He approaches each jump with an eagerness, his ears are pricked and his eyes shining bright. He is athletic and powerful. It goes without saying that Ben and Doc end up cantering around the arena in front, with a rosette fluttering on his bridle. Their rosette is much bigger and brighter and far more beautiful.

Amber and Alaskan Sky leave us with a lot of hugs and waves, and we make our way home. What a wonderful day. I hope that there will be more of those.

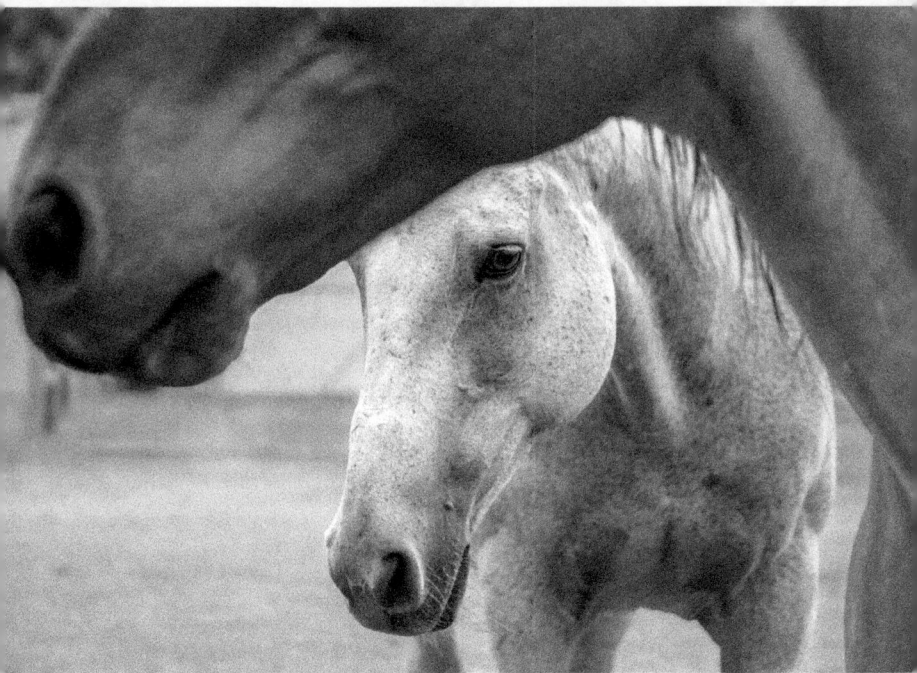

Chapter 16 – A Family of Friends

He knows when your heart is beaming,
He knows when you are feeling low;
He also knows there are carrots in your pocket!

AUTHOR UNKNOWN

A couple of weeks after the show, Doc brings two ladies around to the paddock gate. We all amble over to them to see if they have any treats, and to see what is going on. Okay, so we are a just a bunch of nosy beggars! Of course, Chaps trots ahead; he is always looking for extra. We have all come to realize that girls are the biggest spoilers. They always make more fuss and have lots of treats. We are not disappointed today. As we munch happily on the carrots and apples, Doc tells them our stories and how each of us came to her.

"This is Soldier Boy; he has had an extremely hard life. He will only leave here as a companion horse. I think he has had enough of being ridden and worked."

Doc turns and picks up halters that are lying in the grass behind her.

"Let's tack up, then we can go and ride out a bit."

Ben, Chaps and I are collected in for the ride. I have been out with Chaps a few times; he is a bright and busy horse, and his rider always has a very active ride.

The two visitors are Sheryl and her daughter Bianca. They are both experienced horsewomen and are keen to take us out on the farm. Before tacking up, all three of the ladies come into my stable. Bianca and her mom examine me thoroughly. Sheryl feels along my back and checks my quarters. They check each of my legs, lifting them up and flexing the joints. They take note of the big scars and swellings. They check my feet; Doc tells them how badly they had been worn away. When he is not helping save horses, Victor is a farrier by trade - an expert. It is through careful and patient work that he finally got my feet to the stage where they no longer bother me. Doc takes me onto the concrete walkway and trots me up and down so the two can check my soundness and action. My back and my legs also no longer bother me.

As Bianca tacks me up, she teases her mom about taking the smaller horse. There is a lot of bantering and laughter as the three ladies prepare for the ride, and soon we are on our way. It is such a fun ride; we do quite a bit of jumping and a fast gallop up the hill. Bianca is a good rider; she is kind and brave. Chaps has great fun too – his rider Sheryl is just as spunky as he is and the two get up to all sorts of mischief along the way. Doc looks pleased with everyone. By the time we get back to the stables, we are all feeling happily tired and relaxed. Only the talking has not slowed down.

Doc never sells any horses on, but she does re-home, under very strict conditions. Thorough home checks are done and contracts stating strict terms and conditions regarding the care of the horse are put in place. Frequent follow-up checks are done for every horse that has been re-homed. Horses can be removed from those who do not comply to the requirements on the contracts. Doc and her team have brought a lot of these horses out of hell itself and helped some from out of the clutches of death. She will not have one of them mistreated or go hungry ever again if she can help it. In a case where a person can no longer keep a horse for whatever reason, the horse is not allowed to be passed on or sold, but must go back to Doc.

Sheryl and Bianca come to collect us a few days later. From all their joking and talking, I gather that Chaps was not originally part of the plan, but Sheryl had enjoyed the cheeky fellow so much that he is now included.

The ladies arrive with their own horsebox, and I can see that Chaps feels very important as he is led up the ramp and into the box. Doc leads me into the horsebox and ties me to the ring.

"Now you be a good boy," she says to Chaps who is already tucking into the hay net. She turns to me and places her kind hands on either side of my face.

"I am going to miss you; you are my very special boy."

I wonder where we are going….. I have the feeling that we will not be back; I can't imagine living anywhere else. How can I be without my darling Doc? I nudge at her pockets and, laughing, she produces a piece of carrot. Of course, Chaps also wants one. As we pull out of the yard, I put my nose through the small window at the top and call out, and there are a few answering calls from the paddock.

The trip is quite long, right through the city and along steep, winding roads. Eventually we come to a stop, the ramp is lowered, and we are backed carefully out. I stand

and look around. The air is fresh; I can smell the salty sea on the breeze. There are white-fenced grass paddocks and a stable yard with large stables. It all looks very fancy, like the farm where I was born. As it is late in the day, we are put straight into our spacious, airy stables, fed and watered, and left to settle in for the night.

The rooster starts crowing before the sun is even up. It seems that all farms have one. Bird calls herald the new day here too, but it is another family of raucous guinea fowl and there are seagulls and other sea birds that add to the morning choir.

Heads pop out over half-doors as we hear the feed door scrape open, and a chorus of neighs joins the bird calls. There are six of us in the stables, and a number of ponies and horses that live out in paddocks with shelters. The sound of whistling comes from the feed-room, as someone begins preparing our breakfast. A memory tries to surface . . . it comes from long ago….. from a time when I had known nothing about the harsh realities and the cruel spins and turns of life.

Bianca arrives to help with the feeding. She walks down the line of horses, checking that there is nothing amiss. She stops and talks to Chaps, then moves on to where I am standing. She pats me on the neck and calls over to the person in the feed-room.

"Morning, Mthunzi, have you seen my new horse?"

A Xhosa man appears at the doorway. He stands and stares at me, then drops the feed scoop and walks to my door. He puts a hand on either side of my face and looks into my eyes.

"Hollers the Dodger!"

Bianca is staring at him in surprise.

"Yes, Hollers the Dodger. You know him?" she asks.

"I know him! He was a champion; he was my friend."

Mthunzi opens my door and puts his arms around my neck. He pats me and strokes me, laughing and beaming with happiness. No one can beam better than Mthunzi. He looks at my scarred coat, my short tail that never grew back, and my legs covered with thick scar tissue.

"What happened to him? Was he in an accident?"

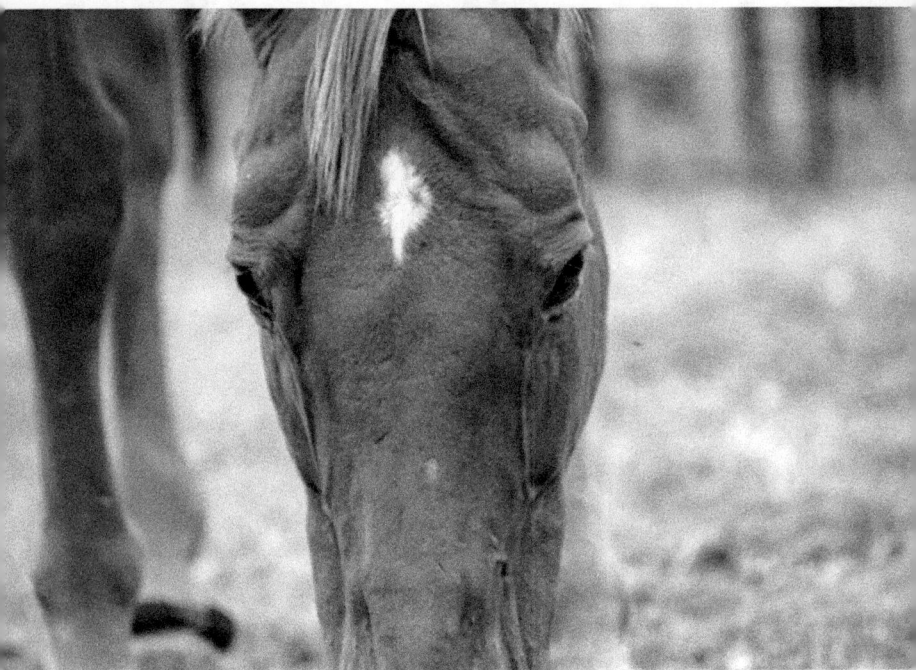

CHAPTER 17 – TREASURES WITHOUT MEASURE

"I am his eyes, He is my wings,
I am his voice, He is my spirit,
I am his human; He is my horse."

AUTHOR UNKNOWN

In the days that follow, Bianca teaches me about groundwork, trotting poles and gymnastics. She teaches me how to move under saddle, how to drop my head and move forward using my hind legs. I find that part quite boring, but I love the jumping that it leads up to. Soon we are deemed ready for a show.

We start with a small training show down the road from us, so Chaps and I are ridden to the venue. It is so much fun! Bianca and I do the first two clear round classes with ease. Sheryl and Chaps are also entered, and they fly around the course like a bullet. As they trot out of the arena the second time, both look very pleased with themselves. On the way home we are taken down a pathway and onto the beach. Chaps has never seen the sea before, but I remember those wonderful times of splashing around in the surf near the racing stables. I go in without hesitation, Chaps follows close behind. We walk for a while in the icy water, feeling the surge and pull of the currents. Then we are trotted back onto the beach, and we wind our way home through the dunes.

My new home is both relaxing and busy. We are well cared for and much loved. Mthunzi and a guy called William are our grooms. Mthunzi has heard as much of my story as Bianca was able to tell him; he was horrified, and he takes special care of his old friend. We are frequent visitors to the beach and go for long hacks up on the mountain tracks.

Bianca is serious about competing and we do a lot of coaching and training. I become muscled and strong. My coat is gleaming. I love the jumping; the more difficult the course, the more I like it. It becomes a challenge to complete it without any mistakes. Even if Bianca makes a mistake, which happens very rarely, I know how to correct myself so we can still jump clear. Sheryl and Chaps jump for fun; Bianca and Hollers jump to win!

Sometimes we see Amber and Alaskan Sky at the shows. In response to the joyful friendship between me and Alaskan Sky, Bianca and Amber have become good friends too (out of the show ring only!). Sometimes Doc comes to see us. She is still my best person.

We are at the National Spring Show. It is huge. The number of horses and riders on the show grounds is quite overwhelming. We have worked up to this day for many months and now that we are here, we wonder why we would ever want to put ourselves through this kind of pressure.

I have been washed, groomed and polished to a high shine. I have been trimmed and oiled. Bianca does not plait my mane; she says that I will need to be able to stretch my neck and use the muscles freely. My mane has been expertly pulled and it is short and neat. My bridle and saddle are clean and shining and I have special boots on to protect my legs from the poles (like I need them – my legs won't go anywhere near those poles!)

Sheryl is pinning Bianca's number onto her black show jacket. Bianca always looks so posh with her show gear on; I feel proud that we are a team. I can see she is very nervous this morning. Mthunzi is giving me a final wipe-down with his 'polishing cloth'. I hear a familiar voice and I lift my head up, ears straining forward to catch it.

Doc rounds the side of a tent and makes her way to where we are all standing.

"Phew, Doc!" Sheryl laughs. "Hollers knew you were coming before we even knew you were here!"

"He always does that," says Bianca, smiling.

Doc comes over and pats me on the neck. I greet my darling Doc, not forgetting to check her pockets for my treat. As usual, I am not disappointed. As I crunch on a piece of carrot, I still feel like I am hearing voices that I know. I pick my head up again, stop chewing, and strain my ears forward.

"What is it with you, Hollers? Doc is here; is it Amber and Alaskan Sky?"

"Oh no, it is not them. I know who he can hear." Doc sounds amused.

She waves at a group of people that have appeared from around the parked horseboxes. They wave back in acknowledgment and three children suddenly break away from the group and sprint towards us. Running flat out in front comes a small girl yelling her lungs out.

"Olly! Olly!"

She slams into my legs and wraps her thin little arms around them. She looks up into my face, tears are streaming down her brown cheeks.

"We thought you died!" she says, in her little chirpy voice.

Poppy! I lower my head and blow into her hair. She grabs my cheeks with both her little hands and gives me a big sloppy kiss on my nose. The two boys approach with more restraint. They seem older and thinner; their eyes have lost their sparkle, they seem sad and hardened. But when Joe and Dan grab me around my neck, their faces crumple and they sob brokenly. The rest of the family arrive. Mthunzi is watching with total astonishment clear on his face. Bianca and Sheryl are standing with Doc; they have obviously been told the story and all of them are blowing hard into tissues. Jake's dear, sweet wife Rose joins her children in the tearful, joyful and heart-wrenching reunion, stroking my neck and rubbing my head. She turns and shyly greets the three ladies standing together, and everyone is introduced. The little family have been staying with Rose's parents, out on a farm away from the gangs and the trouble.

"Sherbet!" Biance realizes the time. "We need to warm up – we are on in half an hour!"

There is much fussing and laughter as the huge entourage sees us off. Poppy is waving frantically as we trot off to the warm-up ring. At first it is hard to focus. My heart is full of memories. Bianca takes me into the practice ring and trots me around in different circles and directions. She asks for my attention, and within a few minutes I start focusing on the task at hand. We work quietly, trotting and cantering before she brings me back to a walk. I feel warmed-up and ready to go. The two practice jumps are not small. One is an upright and the other is a spread, which means it is wide as well as high. We approach the jumps at a strong pace, straight and confident. I am listening to my rider, and we sail over the jumps with the ease of an eagle. We don't overdo it. We slow down, walk out through the gate, and we hear clapping and cheering. The three kids are standing to the side with Mthunzi, and Bianca dismounts to great applause.

"Was that the show?" Poppy asks.

"No, that was just practice." Bianca is laughing.

"I need to walk the course now. Why don't you guys go with Mthunzi and Hollers? They will show you where to sit so you can see everything."

"Can we ride Hollers there?"

"You can sit on him when we are finished. He needs to think about his jumping now."

"Yay! Yes, Olly, think about those biiiiiig jumps. Clever, clever Olly!"

Bianca is smiling as she walks off toward the arena, twirling her jumping stick like a jockey.

............My whole world narrows down to the next jump. I do not see the bright colors of the banners. I do not hear the music or the cheering crowd. I hear nothing but the pounding of my hooves on the grass, my rhythmic blowing with each measured stride and the breathing of my rider. I feel the shift of her weight and the give-and-take of the reins. I hear her encouraging voice as we take off and fly. Wind rushes in my ears. I tuck up my front legs to make sure we clear the poles. I make sure my hind legs don't drag as we land. On to the next one. I trust my rider. She knows the course; she shows me where to go. I am completely focused on the task at hand. Jump after jump . . . the track is tight in places, and it is important to pay close attention. The three jumps are in a line. I feel her focus on the last jump as she lines me up to the first. We fly over the first jump, one stride, gather for take-off; and fly again. Two strides . . . the jump ahead is a massive spread. It feels as if she is throwing her heart over that fence. I gather up, my muscles bunch and burn with the effort as we launch, and I throw my heart over after hers. We are airborne. The second we land; she urges me into a gallop. The red finish flag is a blur as we shoot past it.

The reality of my vibrant surroundings crashes down on me. The cheering and whistling of the crowd, the voice coming through the speakers, the flapping of the brightly-colored flags and banners. We canter a circle then Bianca brings me down to a trot with much fussing, patting, and ruffling of my very neat mane.

We compete in two events, and we get a first and a second. The horse that beat us in the second event was nippier around the corners and so beat us by a few seconds. Who else could it have been but my dear friend, my darling Gray Mare – Alaskan Sky! (And Amber, of course.)

Everyone is very proud. The kids help Mthunzi to hose me down, which turns into a bit of a water fight. They insist on using the scraper to wipe off the excess water. Everyone is allocated a part of me to scrape down, which they do with great precision under the critical eye of the other two. They all sit on my back while Mthunzi leads me to the horse box and organizes me some hay and water. He leaves them sitting there on my back, excitedly recounting the entire two courses blow by blow, every jump. I see him smiling as he packs up all the show equipment. Finally, we are ready to load and set off for home.

Doc has already left to go back to the farm. I have discovered that the police called Doc a few days ago to tell her that my owners had been located. Doc and Rose met up, and as Rose is in no position to keep me, she has signed me over to Doc.

Mthunzi lifts the three kids off my back one at a time amid plenty of protest. Bianca kneels down to their level and draws them into a huddle.

"Hollers told me that he wants you to have this," she says.

She puts her hand into her pocket and draws out the big, beautiful rosette. It is made of brightly colored satin, and the long tails have 'Spring Show' and 'First' printed in gold. The central disk has a golden, shiny picture of horse-jumping. I know it means a lot to her; she has worked very hard to be able to add that rosette to her collection. Poppy takes it reverently and the three crowd around to examine this amazing treasure. Their heartfelt thanks are shouted out joyfully and everyone is hugging. Bianca gives them each a large, shiny color photos of us jumping and posing with the rosette. They are clearly over the moon.

"The children and I would like you to have this," says Rose.

She hands an old, well-oiled and repaired halter to Bianca who studies it closely. She sees my name sewn onto the sidepiece, the new shiny flower sticker and the red shiny heart sewn onto the noseband. She sees the lightning bolt and the skull-and-crossbones that have been scratched into the leather.

"Doc gave it to me the day we met. She had cleaned it up and I have replaced what I can. My husband made it. Hollers was wearing it the day we lost him. It will mean a lot to us if you would accept it."

Bianca looks up, and swallows hard.

"Thank you. This is a very special gift."

To get me ready for the trip home, Mthunzi puts a smart sweat-sheet on me, which really impresses the children. Poppy is pleased with my 'dress' but her brothers argue that it is actually a warrior's cloak. With my halter that has a shiny red heart and flower stickers on the noseband along with etchings of lightning bolts and skull-and crossbones, I think they are all right. All three want to lead me up into the horsebox so to keep the peace, Mthunzi leads me up the ramp and into the box. As he ties me to the front, I see three little faces all with big eyes looking through the door in the front of the horsebox. The ramp is closed up behind me and the children each say their good-byes. I know I will be seeing a lot of them in the future. As we pull out, I catch a glimpse of the little family standing together on the road, waving frantically. Little Poppy, clutching the big shiny rosette to her chest, is blowing lots of kisses. I put my nose up to the little window at the top and call out. A faint chorus of 'Olly, Olly' floats back to me as we turn out of the gate and onto the road.

Chapter 18 – A Wonderful Life

"My troubles are all over, and I am at home;
and often before the dreamy fogs have lifted fully from my mind,
I hear the echoes of friends long gone,
feel their smiles settle upon my heart,
I smell a warm and gentle sweetness.

Evening descends, bringing with it the usual bird-song and night sounds. I doze peacefully in my stable. I hear the other horses pulling at their hay; some are sipping at their water buckets. I hear the soft sighs and occasional stamp of hooves. Bianca and her mom have just left the yard. Bianca brushed me down before supper and checked me for any injuries. She gave me plenty of hugs and kisses. She is very proud of me.

My mind is filled with the memories of all the angels who have brought me to the wonderful life I now live. The road has been painfully cruel and very long. Each angel that has crossed my path shows up as a beacon of light along a very dark path.

I think of the day my beloved Gray Mare came across my path. She shines as the brightest star of all. It was she who made me fight to survive. I somehow knew that if I did not pull through, then neither would she. I remember the blank, hopeless look in her eye as we ran alongside each other.

I think of how she flew over those jumps today. I see her swishing her short tail as she cleared jump after jump. After the second event, we cantered around in the victory lap behind her. At the gate, we drew up alongside and I looked into her eye. It was gleaming with life, shining with excitement; and as she looked back at me, there was the fire of challenge.

THE END

Author's Notes and Acknowledgments

Hollers the Dodger came into our lives as an eight-year-old. I thought he had been in an accident when I saw all the scars on his legs and body. When I was told how he came by those scars, I was devastated. Never in my darkest nightmares had I ever imagined that this type of savagery could exist. Hollers, despite the unimaginable cruelty he has suffered at the hands of the monsters, never shows any animosity or distrust toward people. He is the kindest, purest, most gentle soul I have ever had the privilege to know. Every time I think about what he must have gone through, how his sweet nature and innocent heart were abused with such ruthless, evil intent, I feel a bitter rage on his behalf.

I decided to tell a story that would expose the horrors that take place on our very doorsteps.

This story is based on the life of Hollers the Dodger, but I have taken liberties in adding characters and events. The happenings in the racing yards are mostly gleaned from personal experiences. The Good Friday Races do happen and need to be exposed. I have tried to convey the facts as they were told to me. Although I tried to be as accurate as possible, I could not bring myself to write in detail about the death and destruction of innocent lives. I am sad to say that the actual event is a lot worse than is described in this book. I could not bring myself to have any horses die in this book, but in truth the survivors are few.

In Hollers' actual rescue, he was found in that box after being raced. The brutal evidence that he had been raced in the streets was apparent from his hogged mane, his short tail, his feet that had been worn to stubs, his skin that had been scraped off by the hard road surface as if he had come down at speed. His bloodied legs, his skeletal body, and all the other countless wounds, all pointed to the fact that he had been raced and then stuffed into that tiny box. This is where he was found and rescued by St Romnik Equine Rescue. They are the horse guardians, constantly helping those in need and pulling horses out from the clutches of hell itself.

I invented Jake and his family; I felt that poor Hollers (and you, the reader) needed a break from all the unrelenting darkness in his world. Sadly, he did not have that break in real life and his owners went from bad to worse until the day that he was rescued from the brink of death.

Since the day of his rescue, Hollers has known only love and devotion. He did extremely well jumping in competitions.

Grey Mare was not rescued at the same time as Hollers, she was rescued after the Good Friday races a few years later. Her true story is, I am afraid to say, far worse than what is written in this book. Ironically, both Grey Mare and Hollers have ended up together at the same loving home along with other rescues where a true horse angel of the highest order watches over them, and of course Hollers the Dodger is treated like the amazing hero he is.

www.ingramcontent.com/pod-product-compliance
Lightning Source LLC
LaVergne TN
LVHW021515080426
835509LV00018B/2523